A Legacy of Words
Texas Women's Stories 1850-1920

Edited by Ava E. Mills

Doss Books
San Angelo, Texas

Copyright © 1999 by Ava E. Mills
All rights reserved.

Also by Ava E. Mills:
West Texans Remember the Home Front

Library of Congress Catalog Card Number:
98-96325

Publisher's Cataloging-in-Publication Data

Main entry under title: A legacy of words.

Forty-one narratives originally recorded by members of the Federal Writers' Project. Includes bibliographic references and index.
    1. Women—Texas—Biography
    2. Women—Texas—Social conditions
    3. Frontier and pioneer life—Texas
    4. Texas—History
    5. Oral history
I. Mills, Ava E. II. Federal Writers' Project
    HQ1438 .T4L4   1999   305.4
    ISBN 0-9658789-2-9

Published by Doss Books
P.O. Box 62174, San Angelo, Texas 76906

Manufactured in the United States of America

TX 976.406 Leg OF
A Legacy of words : Texas
   women's stories,
   1850-1920 $ 16.95
                    94266670

SEP 2 6 2001

HARRIS COUNTY PUBLIC LIBRARY
3 4028 03906 7823
OF

DISCARD

A Legacy of Words

Courtesy Fort Concho National Historic Landmark, San Angelo, Texas

Unidentified infant dressed in the style of the 1890s.

Contents

Preface vii

Chapter 1. Early Residents 1
Chapter 2. Texas Weather 21
Chapter 3. Frontier Travel 30
Chapter 4. Stories About Outlaws 40
Chapter 5. Kin to Texas Rangers 49
Chapter 6. Civil War Stories 52
Chapter 7. Indian Stories 57
Chapter 8. Hardships 75
Chapter 9. Ranch Life 81
Chapter 10. Town Life 109
Chapter 11. Settlers 114
Chapter 12. Historic Towns 134

Names of Women 165
Map 166-167
Additional Reading 168
Index 169

Preface

Emma Kelly Davenport talks about being courted by a rancher and marrying him in 1878 when she was 14 years old. Elizabeth Roe tells how her widowed mother raised three children and managed a small farm alone in the 1860s and '70s. Mrs. Arthur B. Duncan describes how wonderful it felt to move from a dugout into a "real home."

These women and others, as well as many men, were interviewed by writers employed by the WPA (Works Progress Administration, later the Work Projects Administration) to collect stories for the Federal Writers' Project. One of several New Deal programs implemented by President Franklin Delano Roosevelt, the Federal Writers' Project collected oral life histories of ordinary people.

When interviewed in the late 1930s and early '40s, the women in this book did not discuss the Great Depression that was winding down at the time of the interviews; they spoke of earlier times, instead. Some told stories that had been passed down in their families, including stories about the Civil War, which they usually referred to as the War Between the States.

Others described their own experiences in the 19th and early 20th centuries. The accounts in this book reveal what it was like to live in Texas during that time.

While most of the stories are first-person narratives, many were written in third person by the WPA interviewers. Stories included here are in their original forms.

Although the focus of this book is on the Texas women who were interviewed and on what they had to say, the WPA interviewer is named at the beginning or end of each story.

The principal editing of these stories involved checking the spelling of proper names. Many errors, primarily in spelling and capitalization, have been corrected. For example, a small town in Texas, "Colombus," now reads "Columbus," while "registered Black Pole cattle" has been changed to "registered black polled cattle." (Black and polled [meaning "without horns"] are descriptive words, and, therefore, not capitalized; the name of the breed was not given.)

The editor has inserted explanatory material in brackets within the text, rather than in footnotes or endnotes, for the convenience of the reader.

None of the stories in this book have been previously published, as far as the editor has been able to determine.

Originals of most interviews were sent to the Library of Congress, where they are now located in the Manuscripts Division, WPA Federal Writers' Project Collection. Participating states retained copies of narratives from their states. The largest collection of Texas narratives is found at the Eugene C. Barker Texas History Center at the University of Texas in Austin.

"By preserving a written record of personal stories, Federal Writers offered men and women the hope that their voices might be heard by an audience beyond their immediate circle of family and friends, and that their lives would touch people they had never met," wrote Ann Banks in the Introduction to her book, *First-Person America*, one of several anthologies based on the Federal Writers' Project.

CHAPTER 1
Early Residents

Mrs. Hattie Vance
Hillsboro, Hill County, near Dallas

Mrs. Hattie Vance has lived on South Waco Street, Hillsboro, since 1887. Left a widow, she became a dressmaker during the period of leg-o-mutton sleeves, bustles, and trains. Dresses were made of alpaca or taffeta, stiff enough to stand alone and "fit like a glove."

The streets were unpaved; the dust in dry weather was ankle deep and the mud in wet weather was above the shoe tops. Through these streets, carrying their heavy trains, the ladies made their way to church, shopping, or on social calls. The first improvement came when the community bought loads of gravel and built walks from the residence section to town.

The homes were furnished with stiff formality. The long lace curtains spread out on the floor like trains. The carpets were Brussels and rag, and the parlor suites upholstered in red plush.

Mrs. Vance remembers the first automobile seen on the streets of Hillsboro and what a sensation it caused, people running from all directions wanting to see it.

Gladys Marshall
n.d.

A Legacy of Words — Texas Women's Stories 1850-1920

Mrs. Fayette Randal
Waco, McLennan County

Mrs. Randal, 2218 Homan Avenue, Waco, is the daughter of William C. and Ella Walker Patterson. Her grandfather, William C. Walker, came to Waco from Chapel Hill in 1851 and bought 650 acres of land on the Bosque for $2.50 per acre. Part of the land is now under Lake Waco. Walker's Crossing on the Bosque was named for him. He built a home on the land he had bought. He built a brick house in 1851, and this house is still standing. The sills are made of cedar logs and the floors are of cedar planks, all in a good state of preservation. The cedar used in the building was grown on the place. The cedar shingles and the lime used were made on the place, and after eighty-five years the wood is as good as when it was built. The windows were brought by ox team from Houston.

Mrs. Randal has some valuable old papers that are now in the Texas Room at Baylor University.

Anne B. Hill
n.d.

Mrs. Ella Cox
Kerrville, Kerr County,
and San Angelo, Tom Green County

Married at seventeen, Mrs. Cox and her husband lived at Kerrville, where he worked for Capt. Charles Schreiner, "who at that time owned nearly everything in that country." The Coxes moved to San Angelo in 1886, when soldiers were still stationed at Fort Concho. Mrs. Cox was 81 years old when she was interviewed in 1936.

All the hardships of pioneer days did not consist of fighting Indians. When I was a young girl, I lived in Washington County near Brenham and was married there to James Monroe Cox when I was 17 years old. We bought and paid for a

Chapter 1 — Early Residents

small farm there, but after a few years we sold it and moved to Kerrville. This long, long trip was made in wagons, one drawn by oxen and the others by horses. A boy drove our milk cows. We passed through San Antonio, which was then very small and dirty, I thought. All I saw were soldiers and Mexicans, and I was more afraid of the Mexicans than I would have been of Indians.

When we got to Kerrville, Mr. Cox unloaded our stuff in the house and started the next day to San Antonio, to take the men who had helped us move, back that far, as he had promised to do when we left Washington County. My husband left with me $1500, as he did not want to take it with him. I didn't know what to do with that money. I put it first one place, then another, and finally at night put it into my shoe. Then in the night I thought that rats or mice might get it, so I held it in my hands all night and was thankful I didn't have any more.

When Mr. Cox came back, he went to work for Captain Schreiner, who at that time owned nearly everything in that country. Captain Schreiner was a fine man, always helped everybody in anyway he could.

Our place at Kerrville was on the Guadalupe River. One side of the cow pen was the bank of the river. We had a windlass to let a bucket down into the river and drew up our water that way. I used to milk the cows in that pen, and in those days when I was young and silly, I used to wish that all the cows would fall over that bluff into the river.

I was afraid to leave the children in the house, so would bring them out and let them stay on the fenced side of the pen.

My husband decided that we would come to this country [at San Angelo], and we moved here in 1886. The soldiers were here in the fort [Fort Concho], and there was very little town. We lived in a tent on our place north of town until we could get lumber hauled from Abilene to build a house.

Mr. Cox took contracts for building fences and would be gone for weeks at a time. I could work in the day, but at night I would be scared almost to death. I remember one night a drunk man rode up to the gate and started to get down. I was watching out the window. Our watch dog, Bull, would stand in the yard until the man would get nearly off, then old Bull would run under the fence, and the man would climb back on his horse. After several attempts, the man went on.

The two oldest boys would have to go across from home to Red Bluffs on Red Creek to drive the milk cows home. The wolves used to get after them. I remember one time the boys were coming along home with old Bull walking with them. When the wolves would get too close, Bull would chase them away. The boys thought it funny, but it wasn't to me.

I was glad when things were more settled. I have never objected to taxes, for we have so much better roads and other comforts. I have always enjoyed train trips. I liked the long one when I went to California several years ago. I like to ride fast in an automobile and may ride some day in an aeroplane.

Miss Nellie B. Cox
January 5, 1936

Mrs. Arthur P. Duggan
Littlefield, Lamb County

Some of Mrs. Duggan's friends in Dallas predicted that she would not stay in the Littlefield area overnight, but Mrs. Duggan said that "when she got one whiff of the breeze that blew over the prairie and took one look at the sky, she knew she would be content to call this new country her home."

Mrs. Arthur P. Duggan and her husband, the late Arthur P. Duggan, were the first residents of Littlefield, Texas, and Mrs. Duggan was the first woman to call Littlefield her home. Mrs. Duggan and her two children joined Mr. Duggan on the plains in the fall of 1912, coming from Dallas.

Some of her friends predicted that she would not stay overnight, but according to Mrs. Duggan, when she got one whiff of the breeze that blew over the prairie and took one look at the sky, she knew she would be content to call this new country her home. Mrs. Duggan said she pitched her tent where the grass was the greenest, speaking of the spot the Duggan home now occupies.

Their first home was a one-room house with a lean-to that

Chapter 1 — Early Residents

the cowboys moved in from the south camp of the Yellow House Ranch. They scoured it with lye and painted it a "sky blue pink," and there the family started its pioneer days. These early citizens of this little town never knew who their next guests would be, because there was much traveling in every direction in those days, and many interesting people were entertained in the Duggan home.

Mrs. Duggan, upon arriving to take up her home in this country, wanted to know which cow they were to milk. Imagine her surprise when her husband informed her that the cows were much too wild to milk, and that they would have to send back to Dallas for their own milk cow. Mrs. Duggan considered this a peculiar circumstance to encounter in a cow country.

The new house that the Duggans built was finished July 4, 1913. One Negro hauled from Lubbock all of the lumber that went into the house. He used a wagon and eight mules. The salt cedar that now borders the Duggan property was brought in from one of the Yellow House camps, and Mrs. Duggan trimmed it and set it out herself.

Marjorie Key
n.d.

[Editor's Note: Mrs. Duggan later moved to Austin. Additional information about her may be found in *Texas Women of Distinction*, by Ina May Ogletree McAdams, published in 1962 by McAdams Publishers, Inc., of Austin.]

Mrs. G. J. (Sula) Nunn
Amarillo, Potter County

Mrs. Nunn knew Col. Charles Goodnight and taught music at Goodnight Academy, established by Col. and Mrs. Goodnight. She talks about other schools in the Amarillo area, including the Amarillo Academy, established by her husband, Dr. G. J. Nunn; Clarendon College; Hereford College; the Canadian Academy; and the Lowrey-Phillips School. Dr. Nunn left the education field to work in real estate, developing the Edgefield Addi-

tion in Amarillo. Mrs. Nunn was living at 1619 Tyler, Amarillo, when the interview took place.

January 1, 1904, Mrs. Nunn came with her husband, the late Dr. G. J. Nunn, pioneer educator of the Panhandle, to Amarillo, where they set up housekeeping at 701 Jackson, in the building which was formerly the first Methodist church in the town, and in which the first religious services for other denominations were held. Since its use as a church building, the house had been remodeled and converted into an apartment house. Mrs. Nunn still recalls with a shudder the "granite" wallpaper with which every room in the building was decorated.

In January, shortly after their arrival, Dr. Nunn established the Amarillo Academy in his home. Students from out-of-town roomed and boarded in the same building. In the summer of 1904 he bought a downtown building which he moved to the academy grounds and used for school purposes. Soon the purchase of another building was required by the growing student body — an old paint shop which was moved to a new location at 705 Monroe Street. This building was utilized as a dormitory for boys attending the academy and was also occupied by the primary department of the school. Boys took their meals in the Nunn home at 701 Jackson, where girl students stayed. After the academy was closed, the building at 701 Jackson was sold and converted into a rooming house which later burned.

Dr. Nunn, who had dabbled in real estate more or less before entering the professional field, carried on this business intermittently while he was teaching in Amarillo, finally giving up school work to devote his entire time to the real estate enterprise, which was more profitable than the educational field.

During the first term of the academy, Dr. Nunn and his wife did the teaching, Mrs. Nunn taking charge of the music and helping with the intermediate work, while her husband taught the higher subjects. The following year W. B. Quigley, who died in May 1935, was added to the faculty. The late Dr. David Fly also taught at one time in the old academy.

The first graduating class was composed of Morris and

Chapter 1 — Early Residents

Mary Browning, Bill Herring's sister, and others. One of Mrs. Nunn's first pupils, whom she taught spelling and grammar or arithmetic, was Bascom Timmons.

Miss Laura Buchanan of the academy's art department did the covers of Holland's Magazine for several years.

As Sula Orr, Mrs. Nunn came to teach in the old Goodnight Academy in 1901, taking charge of the music department a year before Dr. Nunn, who was then president of Polytechnic College in Fort Worth, came to assume the presidency of the college at Goodnight.

Dr. [Marshall] McIlhany, to whom Dr. Nunn had gone to school and under whom Mrs. Nunn had studied as a young girl of fourteen in Stephenville, was one of the founders of Goodnight Academy and persuaded his former pupil to come to the young plains institution. In 1902 Dr. Nunn took charge of the college established by the philanthropic Colonel Goodnight and his wife, who was a school teacher before she married the colonel.

In the summer of 1903 Miss Orr and Dr. Nunn were married, coming to Amarillo in January of the following year.

The Goodnight Academy at the time was still housed in the old church building. The boys' dormitory had two stories, known as the "Upper and Lower Dives."

Clarendon College was evidently older than the Goodnight institution, although the latter is often spoken of as being the oldest college in the Panhandle, because, as Mrs. Nunn recalls, the buildings of the former were of older, substantial brick construction. [Note: Both institutions were founded in 1898, according to the *Handbook of Texas*.]

Contemporaries of the Panhandle college were the Amarillo, Clarendon, Goodnight, Hereford, and Canadian institutions, with perhaps a few years difference in their beginning and ending. The oldest home in Canadian was formerly one of the Canadian Academy buildings. Addison R. [Randolph] Clark was president of the Hereford College, as Mrs. Nunn recalls.

The Lowrey-Phillips School was established in the building which is now [in 1938] occupied by the Children's Home after the Nunn college closed. Mrs. Bertha MacGregor of 1004 Harrison taught a kindergarten about this time.

In the course of his real estate operations, Dr. Nunn, perhaps as early as 1904, acquired a part of the farm which was later developed as Edgefield Addition to Amarillo. Later, the whole of the farm was added to his holdings. Early in the development of this property, Dr. Nunn brought a Dallas realtor to Amarillo to put the acreage on the market, several lots being sold in it at the time, many of which were paid for, others reverting to the owner, Dr. Nunn. About 1926 in the expansion days of the oil boom, the addition was formally opened, streets laid off, lots put up for sale, and the project promoted to a greater extent than in the first venture. The addition was named by the Dallas agent who promoted the first sale of lots in the addition, perhaps because the land had been farm field on the edge of the town.

Mrs. Nunn remembers some of the old buildings of early Amarillo which are still [in 1938] doing service in the town. The H. B. Sanborn home, formerly on the block now occupied by the Municipal Auditorium, now stands at 1311 Madison, in the same condition, except for a coat of paint, green and white, to replace the original yellow. The coach house in which Sanborn kept his tally-ho still stands, converted into a dwelling. The old office building in which he worked was also moved away to an uncertain location, but both coach house and office are parts of other buildings in Amarillo today.

The first Amarillo public school building, the former frame courthouse which served Potter County before the first brick structure was erected, stands at the corner of Ninth and Van Buren streets. The old schoolhouse has been changed until the only thing of its former shape and appearance left are two of the tall, old-fashioned schoolroom windows to help identify it.

Mrs. Nunn recalls an interesting incident in connection with her association with the late Colonel Goodnight. Once when she was showing visitors from out of the state over the Goodnight ranch in the Palo Duro Canyon, she drove a new car with great trepidation in the wake of the irascible old colonel, who led the way across the trackless pastures with a curt, "Turn left" or "Turn right," never looking back to see if the inexperienced driver could follow where his horse went, down a road only wide enough to permit the careful passage of a vehicle. Mrs. Nunn drove her car down a declivity at the bottom of which was a sandy arroyo, where the motor immediately stalled in the sand, refusing to budge any farther.

The impatient old cattleman rode back to see what was detaining her, exclaiming, "Any good driver could have made it. Why didn't you give it the gun?" Wheezing from the asthma which was aggravated by his exasperation, he went over and sat down on a nearby hillside, from which his stentorious breathing could be painfully heard by the occupants of the car, who went in search of the nearest telephone to call someone to come after the stalled automobile, which Mrs. Nunn refused to attempt to extricate from the sand.

Later, Mrs. Nunn, who was a sincere friend of the old plainsman, joked with Colonel Goodnight about the scare he gave her with the stalled car, his asthma, which she feared would be the death of him any minute, and his gruffness.

Unidentified interviewer
June 28, 1938

Mrs. Annie Shaw
Mart, McLennan County, and San Antonio, Bexar County

Mrs. Shaw was living in San Antonio and visiting in Mart, her former home, when she was interviewed.

We had relatives who had already moved to Texas and were urging my father [William Woodward] to come. They were Frank Foster of Mart; my aunt and her family, Mrs. Ben Reynolds of Mart; and [Uncle] Will Hartsfield of Milam County, near Calvert. All these had written glowing descriptions of the country, and so we were filled with the desire to try our fortunes in this new land, and especially were my brothers interested. They were filled with the spirit of adventure, and the hope of the rich and cheap land was also a factor of my father's decision to come to Texas.

We came by way of Atlanta, Georgia, and New Orleans. Crossed the Mississippi River on a ferry boat and on through

South Texas to Waco. Our tickets were over the new Houston and Texas Central Railroad, and we were at the little place they called Harrison Switch, about ten miles south of Waco, when to our surprise our relatives, Mr. Foster and Reynolds, met the train and brought us on to the little village of Mart. We came in the wagons on the 16th day of December, 1884.

Their object in taking us off the train was in order for us to be in time for a wedding of a cousin, Ada Reynolds, and Jack Payne. This was an important affair to the ones concerned. The relatives and the neighbors were there in large numbers, and the house was filled to overflowing. Old Brother Hardwick, one of Mart's first preachers, was the officiating minister.

This wedding occurred at the old Lewis Stephens place, now owned by Dr. J. R. Gillam of Mart, about two or three miles northeast of Mart. It was in December, and so we had Christmas decorations. There was a reception after a most bountiful dinner, which was partaken of by around a hundred guests. The guests would eat in groups, as there was not enough room at the table for all at a time. There were all kinds of good things to eat, and truly we felt that Texas was a place where we would not go hungry. The next day the father and mother of the groom gave an "infair" and served dinner to the bridal couple and the relatives.

We rode to it in wagons, and the bride and groom rode horseback. The bride's horse had a sidesaddle on which she sat sideways. It would have been a shocking thing for the ladies to have ridden astride, as the custom is now. She had on a long riding skirt which extended below her shoes. If she had fallen off the horse, her feet would have become tangled up in the skirt.

As we had just arrived from Georgia, where it was a timbered country and everyone had their carriages and buggies, the change to riding on the open prairie in an open wagon, and the ladies riding horseback, the contrast was noticeable, to say the least, to us. I had never seen a sidesaddle before, and I did not understand how one could stay on one without falling.

Over in the present cemetery at Mart was where the little house stood that was used for a church and school combined. That was the first school and church house in the community. As I understand it, the first school was taught

Chapter 1 — Early Residents

for three months by a Mr. Spickard in the year 1879, with an enrollment of fifteen pupils. The winter of 1880, Mrs. Laura Cowan, who was our neighbor when we came to Mart and whom we learned to honor and love, taught the next school with an enrollment of twenty-eight.

In the winter of 1885 and 1886, a Mr. and Mrs. Chambers taught in this same school house. I was a pupil, and by this time there were many more children in the community. As well as I can remember, there were around fifty pupils. I do not recall all the names of the families who were represented, but some of them were the Howards, Reynolds, Stephens, Ingrams, Tulls, Barron, Criswell, Vaughan, Suttles, Lumpkin, and I think Mrs. Cowan's oldest child, E. J., was one of the pupils; also the Dunn boys, Rogers, and Valentines.

When the winter term closed, Mr. Chambers got up a private school, and I assisted him to pay for my tuition. I was fifteen years of age at the time and was still anxious to keep up with my studies. I have since taught in the State school, but was never so proud of any school as this, my first experience under my teacher and with my neighbors' children for my pupils.

When we came to the Mart community in 1884, we rented land from an old bachelor by the name of Brooks. The country was a ranch and stock country. The men raised their grain, but not until a few years later did they commence to raise cotton. Our landlord owned ranches and city property in Waco, but was a confirmed old bachelor. Many were the stories told of why he did not get married. One was that he took a barrel, and every time he would eat a meal he would throw an equal amount in the barrel. At the end of the month, when he looked into the barrel, he said that it would break any man to feed a woman, and he dared not try it!

We lived on what is now the Eskew Dairy place, about half-a-mile north of Mart. To the south of us there lived the Townsend family, who were among the first settlers, and to the east, across the road, was the family of Mr. and Mrs. H. C. Cowan whom I have mentioned, Mrs. Cowan being the second teacher to teach the Mart school. Better neighbors could not be found, and many times their neighborly kindness helped us in sickness and in our trials of the new country to readjust ourselves to the new life. There is a fond place in my memory for these our nearest neighbors.

Mart was a little village with the stores situated on a public road on what is now South Carpenter Street, at the intersection of the street which turns off to the present school house. There were three or four stores—that of W. B. Stodghill—Ward Hewin was working for Mr. Stodghill, but later owned a business of his own. Mr. John Pearce was a clerk in one of the stores. Also J. W. Howard, who operates a grocery today in Mart, Mart's oldest grocery man.

Captain Patillo from Waco was the Postmaster, and Dr. R. L. Smith, now of Waco, was just beginning to practice medicine. Then there was Dr. Carpenter and Dr. Stephens. The ministers I remember best were Brother Suttle and Hardwick, who lived in Mart until their passing to the great beyond.

In 1900 I married Sam Shaw and moved to Henrietta, Texas. That was still an unsettled or thinly settled country, and the stock- and ranchmen had drifted farther west from Central Texas. We did not like it there; it was so open and the winds blew so hard, so we moved to New Mexico and took up a government claim, which we still own. But the winds were so high and the sand would drift so badly that we found it not to our liking, and so we came later to San Antonio, where we found the climate much more to our fancy, much milder winters, and here my husband has been in business and we reared our children.

We had three girls, who are now married and have homes of their own. They are Mrs. Ethel Fisher of Fredericksburg, Mrs. Irene Gipson of El Dorado, Arkansas, and Mrs. James Martin of San Antonio.

We love our home and our neighbors and church in this city [San Antonio], but the dearest place in our hearts were the kind friends and neighbors in the little village of Mart, who helped us to adjust our lives when we came to Texas and found it so different in its unsettled condition from our home back in Georgia. These people also had left their homes in the old states and were among the best friends and neighbors we ever had the good fortune to find.

Miss Effie Cowan
n.d.

Chapter 1 — Early Residents

Mrs. M. B. Willis
Waco, McLennan County

Mrs. Willis' husband and father-in-law were prominent physicians in Waco, and her son was a judge.

My parents, Mr. and Mrs. Moses Baldwin, were natives of Alabama. They grew up in the same town. Both married; my mother marrying a Mr. Davis. After a few years my mother's first husband died. She left Alabama and went to live in Mansfield, Louisiana, where she met my father, whose wife had also died, and a year after the meeting they were married.

My father and mother decided to leave Louisiana and come to Texas. They, with my two half-brothers and two half-sisters, children by my father's previous marriage, with about one hundred slaves, went directly to Cold Springs, San Jacinto County, Texas, where my father bought a very large farm. Two years after they had settled in Cold Springs, I was born, November 8, 1855. I was named Armanda, but since that was also my mother's name it was shortened to "Mannie," and Mannie I have remained all my life.

My childhood was very happy. My niece, daughter of my half-sister, and I were almost the same age, and I remember that my father gave each of us a girl slave who was about our own age. It was the custom to give each child a slave near their own age so they could grow up together. There were also "mammies" who had the complete charge of us. My own brother, who was a year or so older than I, also had a slave. We children were taught at home until we were old enough to go to school in Cold Springs. There was no school for the slaves. Whatever they learned, they learned from us.

I cannot remember much about the [Civil] War. My two half-brothers fought in it, but my father's health was so bad that he could not take an active part.

I remember very distinctly one morning going into the dining room and seeing on the dining table stacked piles of silver dollars. My father and mother were standing at the head of the table and grouped around were the heads of the families of slaves.

He was explaining to them that the war was ended and that they were free and could leave if they so desired, but if they wanted to stay and work on, he would give them a contract. Just two of them decided to leave, the coachman and my mother's seamstress, whom she had favored more than any of the others.

The following spring my father died, and my mother had a trying time. The farm was so large, and people began coming to our farm and hiring the Negroes.

The following year we began to attend school in Cold Springs. My brother would take me with him on his horse. It was through his teachings that I became a fine horsewoman. As we grew up, horseback riding was our chief sport, and our next favorite past-time was the game of croquet and dancing, though my mother would not let me attend many dances, as she thought too-frequent attendance would make a young lady common.

Upon finishing school in Cold Springs, I was sent to Waco to attend what was then Waco University, which began quite an interesting period in my life. I was clever but not very studious. Our recreation in those days was picnics, and it was at one of these given on the Baptist Encampment grounds that my husband first saw me. He told the boys that some day soon he was going to know me. Then came a big event—a grand soiree was given, and it was there we met.

A few days later Professor Burleson announced in chapel that we were to be given a big picnic, but there was not to be any pairing off. If anyone was caught disobeying that rule, they would be sent home. There were about six couples including Mr. Willis and myself who were very much in love, and we determined not to let a rule interfere with us being together. So after arriving on the picnic grounds, and at the first opportunity, we slipped off. Mr. Willis took me to the bank of the creek where he had hidden some ice cream, and we were sitting there eating it and having a lovely time, when Professor Burleson walked up and caught us. In a very stern manner he said, "Miss Baldwin, you are to return home immediately, and are not to have any dinner." When I got to the bus, which was driven by Perry Green, I found that the other girls had been caught, too, and were being sent home from

Chapter 1 — Early Residents

the picnic. In some way the boys reached home before we did, and Mrs. Caldwell, who was then Molly Hayes, felt so sorry for us that she fixed up a nice dinner and invited the boys to join us. So we had a nice time in spite of Professor Burleson.

In June I returned home and in a few days Mr. Willis came to my home and asked my mother for her consent to our marriage. My brother had made investigations and found that he was a splendid young man of sterling worth, son of a prominent physician in Waco, who had been in practice with his father for a little more than a year. He had been educated in Virginia and Washington, where he had won the Greek Certificate and was given a beautiful letter from General Lee commending him for his outstanding work. Leaving Washington, he attended Bellview Medical College in New York where he took his medical course, graduating with high honors.

In November we were married, and after a short honeymoon spent in Galveston, we came to Waco which was then known as Waco Village. It was very crude but the people were friendly. Our first home was a little cottage located out on South Fourth Street. It faced open prairie.... Another thing that gave the old settlers quite a lot of pleasure was the theater parties. We often gave them at the old Garland Theater which was one of Waco's leading theaters in those days, even though it was built over a livery stable.

The suspension bridge was also a great event for Waco. The crossing of the river had been accomplished in a flat boat since the settlement of Waco. The ferry was at the same spot where the bridge now stands, and the sight admired by thousands who crossed on that ferry was the beautiful Waco Spring. It used to fall over two shelves of rock, a miniature cataract [waterfall], of two or three yards in width, glittering in the morning sun like a sheen of diamonds. There were no water companies and the spring was free to all.

We had five children; they came very rapidly. One died in infancy. My husband died at the age of 37, leaving me the responsibility of rearing four babies. The youngest was two years old and the oldest ten years old. Being a firm believer in education, I was determined with the help of God to have my children thoroughly educated. Each of my children have from two to three degrees to their credit.

I have been quite active in the religious, civic and social life of Waco. I was one of the organizers of the Home Association of Waco (Old Ladies' Home). I have been quite active in club work and am an honorary member of the Literary Club. When in Waco I attend the Austin Avenue Methodist church. I divide my time between my daughter who lives in Bryan, Texas, and my son, Judge J. D. Willis, of Waco. Life has given me many blessings for which I am most thankful.

Mrs. Edgerton Arnold
n.d.

Mrs. H. E. Chestnut
Amarillo, Potter County

Mrs. Chestnut lived at 1406 Monroe Street in Amarillo.

As a small child, Mrs. Chestnut came to Amarillo with her parents, Mr. and Mrs. Trigg, in 1899. Mr. Trigg brought his wife, who had a chronic throat ailment, to the High Plains for her health, which she regained in the salubrious air of the Panhandle.

Mrs. Trigg, wearied with the long overland journey and dismayed at the dreary stretch of unadorned prairie, asked her husband if he were going to the "jumping off place."

When the Trigg family arrived in Amarillo, the famous Amarillo Hotel was still in the process of construction. The best residential district at that time was in the vicinity of First and Fifth streets, on Lincoln, Pierce, and Buchanan. Streetcars later ran south on Lincoln to Fifteenth and thence to Washington.

The home of W. D. Twichell, pioneer teacher and educator of Amarillo, was at 710 Pierce, as Mrs. Chestnut recalls, where he taught a private school. Mr. Twichell, who was one of the first surveyors in Amarillo and the Panhandle, stayed in Tascosa during the most hectic period of that notorious old cowboy capital.

Mrs. Chestnut remembers the time when the first church house in Amarillo, the old Methodist church building at 701

Jackson, was used by all local denominations in friendly cooperation. The presiding ministers of the first Amarillo churches frequently eked out a slender income by going into the outlying districts of the Panhandle to hold services.

Famous Heights Park, created about the lake still to be seen south of the Tenth Street Highway, was established by a Mr. Isaacs who owned the Famous Dry Goods store in Amarillo, as Mrs. Chestnut remembers. Mr. Isaacs built an island in the middle of the lake, connected to the mainland by means of an earthen causeway. A pavilion on the island provided shade and a place for dancing or band playing. Boats were operated on the lake, which was reached by an open bus. The Isaacs' home, a neat brick structure, still stands east of the lake.

Mrs. Chestnut remembers the time when the rangers were stationed in Amarillo between Fourth and Fifth streets on Tyler. John L. Sullivan was one of the rangers whose name she recalls. Rangers were needed to keep order, for cowboys, after long drives from distant ranches of the Southwest and even old Mexico, gave themselves over to relaxation and the pleasures of the town's numerous saloons. Trail herds were often held on the prairie near Amarillo in the vicinity of the stockyards, which were located on the present site of the shelter.

Mrs. C. M. Cohea
n.d.

Mrs. T. C. Brown
Amarillo, Potter County

Mrs. Brown lived at 1605 Hillcrest Street in Amarillo.

I came here 35 years ago [in the early 1900s]. I did not go to school here, but I did go to school in Clarendon. When I first came, I worked for Mr. Levy, who had the first real department store in Amarillo. It was located at 501-3-5 Polk Street. He came here just as a young man and went into business. He was an Alysesch Jew and had a charming personality. He was a good manager and prospered.

I also worked at White-Kirk's. It was located where Harry Holland's now is, at Fifth and Polk streets.

When I first came here, saloons were still here, but the people voted local option. The women didn't vote, of course, so I didn't pay too much attention to the election.

There was no paving at all and none was put in until 1911.

The Elks Club was the first show place of Amarillo. It was the nicest place of its kind between Dallas and Denver. There was the Deandi Theatre on Taylor Street, across from the new post office (west), and the Grand Opera House, which was at Seventh and Polk. It later burned down, but I was away at that time.

Dust wasn't so bad then. Of course, the wind blew and there was some dust, but nothing like it is now. I think that was due to the pastures. All that's under cultivation now and causes more dust than if it were a pasture.

There was lots of snow. 1918 and 1919 were the coldest winters I ever saw.

The old McIntosh Hotel was on Lincoln some place, but I can't remember the number.

I never went to the Clarendon College, but Earnest (Dusty) Miller and his wife are both graduates of that school and should know a great deal of its history. I think Rev. Hardy organized it.

I remember the street cars. There was one that ran out to Glenwood Park. They just ran every 30 minutes. We young folks just thought it awfully hilarious to ride out to Glenwood on Sunday afternoons.

Claudia Harris
n.d.

Mrs. Elizabeth Roe
Azle, Tarrant County

I was born within three miles of where I am now living, on the 6th day of January, 1855.

My father, William Fletcher, owned a small tract of land located on Ash Creek. There was a settlement there called the Ash Creek settlement. This little village of Azle did

Chapter 1 — Early Residents

Courtesy West Texas Collection, Angelo State University, San Angelo, Texas

"Freight train from San Antonio to Fort Concho in 1880."

not exist at the time I was born, but was a part of the Ash Creek settlement.

Even when I was old enough to note events, I do not remember hearing about Fort Worth until a number of years later. Weatherford was the main trading point for us Ash Creek settlers and where we obtained our mail.

A trip to Weatherford was an eventful occasion and usually made on horseback. During my girlhood days, I never saw a buggy. If we desired to go somewhere, we either walked or rode a horse.

If there was a number of people going somewhere together, they would either be mounted on horses or all ride in a farm wagon pulled by oxen or a team of mules.

A short distance from our settlement was located the section where folks depended on only cattle for a living. I recall some of the large cow camps in those days. There were the McLean, Watson, Bill Smith, and John Collins camps in the surrounding territory.

In the Ash Creek settlement, there were no real cow camps, but the settlement was surrounded with cattle ranches, and many of the settlers, especially the young men, worked more or less as cowhands on the adjacent range.

The village of Azle did not get started until I was a young woman. I do not recall the year, but it was during the Civil War, as I recall about the close of the conflict.

The village received its start when Dr. Stewart located here with his family. He attended the sick in this section and operated a farm, which was located at the east edge of the present village. He died here about 30 years ago.

After Dr. Stewart located in the community, a man named Moore opened a store. He put in a small stock of goods and conducted his business in a little log cabin. Later, Joe Fowler bought Moore's store. Fowler enlarged the business.

Then, the next step towards a village was the location of a post office here, which was operated in connection with the store. Finally, a blacksmith shop was started, then another store. This amount of business remained the business section of Azle for a number of years. After the automobile came in general use, gas stations, garages, and sandwich shops opened up.

This settlement, except for Azle, has not changed much since I was a young woman. Of course, there is more land under cultivation, and the houses are now frame structures.

Sheldon F. Gauthier
n.d.

CHAPTER 2
Texas Weather

Mrs. Belle Little
Mart, McLennan County

A Cyclone and More

Texans had a saying that no one but fools and newcomers prophesied on its weather. It has its moods of sunshine and showers, storm and calm.

It was on the 24th day of November, 1896, at four o'clock in the afternoon. My husband was plowing in the field and I was sitting at the machine, sewing. It had been rainy and misty.

Mr. Little rushed in and caught up our younger child, Arthur, age 5, and told me to follow with the eldest, Dora, a child of 12 years. The boy was standing on the front porch and a hammer lay on the floor beside him.

Just as we closed the door of the storm house, we saw the house go. The cyclone came in a dark cloud which seemed to be rolling on the ground from the southwest and covered a path of about half-a-mile.

All we had left after scrapping the lumber from this cyclone was enough to build a little smoke house. Our clothes, furniture, and bedding were carried so far away, all we ever found were pieces which had caught in the treetops as they were carried away by the wind. Left intact were the porch on which the boy was standing and the hammer. Everything else but the storm house and our family were gone.

This was due to the fact that the roof of the storm house is just above the ground and covered with earth. There are very few in this country, as such storms are very rare. They are more numerous in western Texas, since it has more prairie country and more storms.

Our house and the house of my cousin, Buck Douglass, were the only houses in this cyclone's path. His house was destroyed, also, and his little child killed by the chimney falling on it. They escaped with their lives, by leaving the house when the cloud came, but in the excitement the little child ran under the chimney of the house, when it had reached the outside, and was killed.

The cyclones were not all we had to contend with in those days. I can remember how the grasshoppers came in the fall of 1873, and how they ruined the vegetation. Previous to this, it is a historical fact that they came in 1853, 1857, and 1868. After three days the vegetation looked as if a fire had swept over it. They even got into the houses and clothing.

Then the drouths came and played a big part in the change from ranching to farming, as the grass was killed so that stockmen had to take their stock to other states for range. It is said that from 1859 to 1861 there was scarcely any rain in Texas for three years. As the country was put into cultivation, the drouths gradually ceased, until now they are never so bad that we have a complete failure.

Notwithstanding the drouths, frosts, cyclones and insects, the climate of Texas as a whole, since I have lived here, cannot be surpassed. When the spring comes with its accompaniment of Texas winds and gentle showers, the wild flowers springing up over the prairie with their riot of color, while flinging their fragrance far and near, carry anew nature's age-old message of the Resurrection.

Fall brings the frost king, who paints his pictures in all his gorgeous shades on every bush and shrub. In the midst of it all sits the yellow goldenrod, which nods serenely as autumn's flower queen. Then winter's chilling blast drives all nature's subjects to seek a long siesta in the cold light of a winter's sun. The wild sumac, the red-bud, and the cedar trees which grow in profusion in the rocky sandy soil west of Waco, when the snow and frost come, make a picture worthy of the greatest artist brush.

Miss Effie Cowan
n.d.

Mrs. A. E. White
Littlefield, Lamb County

The Blizzard of 1918 in Lamb County

Mr. and Mrs. A. E. White, who lived on a farm two miles east of Littlefield, were entertaining friends on a night in January 1918.

The four played "500" until about one o'clock in the morning, and when their guests decided to leave, Mr. and Mrs. White walked to the gate with them. They commented on the beauty of the night. Only a few fluffy, white clouds could be seen in the sky, and the moon was shining brightly.

The family returned to the house, only to be awakened about four o'clock in the morning by the intense cold and the lowing of the cattle. To their surprise, they found snow all over the house; even the beds were completely covered. The house was built of ship-lap and well-papered on the inside, but was of little protection against the driving wind and snow. Mr. and Mrs. White and the children went to work to get the snow out of the house, and in the days that followed, bushel baskets were used to carry it out. They took brooms to the barns and used them to sweep off the cattle. Rain had evidently fallen early in the night, for the cattle were frozen on the side that faced the wind.

The next morning the storm abated. The school truck came by for the children, and two of the boys went, the other two remaining at home with their parents. The truck had been gone only a short time when the snow began to fall again. A few hours later the thermometer read ten degrees below zero. Mrs. White moved the bed and couch close to the stove, and the family went to bed to keep warm. One of the boys made his bed in a large wicker chair. They stoked the stove with coal and tried to keep the house as warm as possible.

The electricity was so great that when one of the boys in a

playful mood touched the stove with one hand and his mother's forehead with the other, it almost pulled the skin off.

Mrs. White became very worried about her two children who had left that morning for school. She wanted to go in search of them, but her husband convinced her that she could not get any place in the storm. In desperation she had about decided to saddle the horse and go after them, when word came that Mrs. T. F. Wright had taken the children to her home in town. Mrs. White appreciated this gesture because they were strangers in this western country, having moved out from Wisconsin the year before, 1917.

Before the storm that lasted three days was over, many cattle froze to death and were found heaped in fence corners. One fine bull that Mr. White had just bought for five hundred dollars had followed the drifting cattle and was found in one of the large piles of dead cattle. As late as [?] evidences of the blizzard could be seen. Heaps of bones could be found on the ranchlands.

One man was found frozen to death near the spot where the town of Shallowater now stands. The man had called at the White farm the afternoon before the storm began. He had on plenty of clothes but they were in a very ragged condition. Mrs. White invited the man to come in, but he told her that he would like to have a little coffee and a can to make it in. Mrs. White told him that she would be glad to make the coffee for him but he refused. She, therefore, furnished an empty tomato can to make the coffee in, and half a loaf of white bread. The man accepted the coffee and bread but declined to come into the house and warm. A short time later his camp fire could be seen. That night the blizzard came, and the next day the same man was found frozen to death.

Mrs. White said that she felt very bad about the man's death. Although she had done her best to get the man to come into the house and accept food and warmth, and he steadfastly refused, Mrs. White said that blizzard was really something to live through. All the years they have lived in and around Littlefield, they have never experienced such cold weather as they did then.

Marjorie Key
November 21, 1936

Chapter 2 → Texas Weather

Mrs. C. F. Jackson
Lubbock County

More on the Blizzard of 1918

My husband was in Kansas looking after some cattle that he had pastured up there, when that terrible blizzard struck West Texas in 1918. We were living on a place that we bought from Jim Brown in 1916. This place was located near Lubbock, but we had a ranch out 20 miles west of Sudan, and when that blizzard came up, the men at the ranch phoned me that the cows were freezing in the pastures.

This ranch consisted of about 2500 acres of land, which belonged to C. S. Smith of Vernon and was leased by my husband. He had it stocked with 2000 head of registered black polled cattle. All of these cows wore chains around their necks with their numbers on them, and records were kept of the birth of new calves and their registration dates. These cows were well cared for, they had sheds and stalls to protect them from the bad weather, but as Mr. Jackson bought, sold, and traded cattle all of the time, he often had quite a drove of common-blooded cattle at the ranch. Of course, these cows were kept in a separate pasture from the black polled, and they had no protection whatever from the cold.

We had never lived on a ranch and I knew nothing about ranch life or the care of cattle, so I simply did not know what to do about the cows. Joe Jackson, my son-in-law, went out there to see what could be done. After a while he phoned me that they had decided to bring the cows that were suffering the worst, but still able to travel, in to our home place. He told me to have plenty of hot water ready for them.

I ran right out and turned the windmill on. As soon as I could, I filled all of the wash-tubs and the pot. It was bitter cold and I could hardly stand to get out in the yard, but I knew that the men would be half-frozen when they got in, so I did what I could and then sat down to wait. After a long time I saw them coming. I will never forget how these poor cows looked when they came hobbling in over the hardened ground. Their legs were frozen from their knees down and were badly swollen. Some of their limbs had burst open, and they left a trail of blood spattered on the icy roads behind them. The cows went lame and got down all over the place, their feet and legs just rotted off. In spite of all that we could do, we lost about 60 of the cows after all of our work and trouble.

Ivey G. Warren
January 7, 1937

Mrs. W. M. Anderson
Durango, Falls County

A Hailstorm, Drouth, and a Cyclone

I came to Durango from Hunt County with my husband in 1873. In 1878 we had a hailstorm which fell with destructive force in late May. Roasting ears, cotton, and oats, which showed fine prospects, were mowed completely down. We had to plant all over again.

Then in 1887 there came a drouth, and things got so desperate that the work animals and stock had to be moved over to Salt Branch, near Cego, where they were kept for two months.

And then a cyclone came! This was in May of 1892. Crops were in good condition, except for the need for rain. Farmers' work all done at the close of the day. We looked at the clouds and thought there would be rain at last, but it was more than rain. Funnel-shaped clouds formed quickly in the northwest above Durango, and there was a whirlwind of dust and debris; then came a roaring, crashing sound. The funnel-shaped cloud swept to the ground in terrific roar and force. It cut a path south-eastward, uprooting trees, tearing up houses and splintering trees. Crops were destroyed, and then it was all over in a few minutes.

The people of Durango awoke to find that a number of their relatives, friends, and neighbors had been killed or wounded. Mr. and Mrs. Tom Weathers were killed with two of their children, almost instantly. Miss Bessie Farmer (sister of Lee Farmer) a young lady in her teens, was mortally injured. Others were injured, some seriously, others less seriously. Many, many marveled at the miracles that happened seemingly to save their lives.

The cyclone swept by the house of Lee Farmer. Fearful of the tragedy, he ran to the home of his parents which was squarely in its path a mile away. He found the house a wreck and his sister badly hurt and suffering. She died next day. The four of the Weathers family were buried in one grave. They were the people of Mrs. Farmer.

Mr. and Mrs. Parnell, who live a few miles east of Durango, saw the whirling wind and the dark cloud. They heard the din and roar of the trees and saw bits of household belongings blowing through the air. This was followed by a heavy rain. They were so impressed by it they put the date in the family Bible—May 30, 1892.

Miss Effie Cowan
n.d.

Becky Sanford
San Angelo, Tom Green County

The Ben Ficklin Flood of 1882

We were living not far from Ben Ficklin [also spelled Benficklin] when it was washed away by the flood. I saw many of the victims brought out of the water. Some were hanging in the trees and others were washed away downstream.

Miss Nellie B. Cox
February 10, 1938

Mrs. C. G. Landis
Amarillo, Potter County

A Flash Flood in Palo Duro Canyon

Mrs. Landis lived at 1119 Jackson in Amarillo.

One of the most exciting experiences [wrote the WPA interviewer] which Mrs. Landis recalls as a newcomer to the plains happened on a trip, her first, to the scenic Palo Duro

A Legacy of Words — Texas Women's Stories 1850-1920

Canyon, where many of the early settlers went in the fall to gather wild grapes and plums, which made delicious jellies, conserves, and deep-dish cobblers. However, Mrs. Landis herself admits, somewhat ruefully, that she never could quite make grape jelly jell.

One day in October of 1892, when the grapes were at their ripest and best, friends of the Landises in Amarillo, who ran a livery stable at the present location of the Grand and Silver five-and-ten store, came out and invited the former to go on a fruit-gathering outing to the Grand Canyon of the Panhandle. The next day the party, starting from the Golither home where the W. H. Fuqua residence now [in 1938] stands, made the all-day drive to the canyon. School was in session, and the Golithers left their children at home, all except the baby. The Landises had their children with them, the youngest now being the jailer at Amarillo. Mr. and Mrs. Landis took quilts and blankets and the Golithers a mattress and bedding for the two nights which they expected to spend in the Palo Duro, the night of their arrival and the second night after the one day of gathering grapes and plums and enjoying the gorgeous view before returning the second day.

Driving down the canyon floor for five or six miles, they selected a suitable spot and pitched camp for the night. While the womenfolks were preparing supper, thunder growled overhead. That night rain came down in torrents. However, the next morning the group went out to find the fruit for which they had made the long trip. The men cut down trees heavily laden with grape vines twisted about their branches and with luscious purple grapes hidden among their leaves.

Stepping across the tiny trickle which was the creek, the women placed the children on a wagon sheet spread upon the sandy "beach" of the Palo Duro Creek. Looking up the canyon, Mrs. Landis beheld a sight which was strange to her uninitiated eyes.

Calling to her friend, she said, "What is that great white mass up the gorge. I can't make out what it is. It looks like snow, but I never saw anything like it before." Mrs. Golither, who was better acquainted with the vagaries of the plains than her friend, took one look at the grayish-white wall towering up the canyon and cried, "A headrise! Run for your lives!"

Mrs. Landis recounts those exciting moments: "We gathered up the young'uns and started for camp across the creek, over which we had stepped but a few minutes before, as fast as we could go, but before we got across, the water was swirling about us waist deep. Mr. Landis and Mr. Golither hurriedly drove the wagon and team upon a higher level where they thought they would be safe from the flood waters, but soon they had to move the outfit to a still higher ledge. For three days and nights we stayed in the canyon, with food only for the one day and the two nights planned for the outing. We had to wait until the water receded enough so that we could find the trail back to the point where we had entered the canyon, as that was the only way out. There were no roads, only cattle trails, in the Palo Duro at the time."

The WPA interviewer added this notation: Headrises are sudden and swift in the deep canyons and ravines of the high plains. A dry arroyo may be a destructive avalanche of water in a mere fraction of time. Had not the floor of the canyon been "spread out" at the point where the outing group was caught, the story might have had a different and tragic ending.

Mrs. C. M. Cohea
March 1, 1938

Mrs. W. H. Downing
Wichita Falls, Wichita County

In 1904 we had a terrible sand storm. Mr. Downing was plowing in the field, and the wind became so strong that it blew him out of the row, so he quit and came in. There were other bad sand storms in those early days; sometimes we could not see the buildings across the street. One storm lasted for three days and nights.

Ethel C. Dulaney
August 19, 1938

CHAPTER 3
Frontier Travel

Mrs. Belle Little
Mart, McLennan County

I was born in Little Rock, Arkansas, on the 3rd of April, 1867. I came to Texas with my parents, J. W. and Sarah Louise Mulloy, in the year 1872. We drove through the country in an old covered wagon with oxen as our team. We crossed the Red River on a ferry boat. I remember that when Father drove the wagon onto the ferry boat, the wagon was so long that it would hardly go on the boat with the oxen, and how the ferry-man swore about it.

When we reached the Navasota River in East Texas, we had to wait two weeks for it to go down, as it was on a rise. We stopped at the old Sterling place. It was a large plantation with its slave quarters; the owner was an ancestor of the ex-Governor Sterling of Texas. The men of the plantation entertained our menfolks by taking them hunting and fishing, while the women were wonderfully hospitable and kind.

When we finally crossed the Navasota River, and after traveling over the as yet untraveled roads over the prairie, after leaving the timbered river bottom, what a beautiful sight met our eyes. As far as the eye could see the prairie of wild grass, it was sparsely covered with a native growth of mesquite trees, and the sage and wild grass intermingled with the Texas wild flowers, the bluebonnet, the red Indian-head, dandelion, wild roses, and many others, made a picture to satisfy the eye of an artist. When our pioneers, urged on by the restless spirit of adventure, gazed on the prairie, they could not pass it by. It was a land of promise, beautiful with its carpet of wild flowers and rich in fertility of soil, running streams, and an abundance of wild game.

By the side of the Tehuacana Hills, there were the cool springs. As the shadows of a long, hot day was lengthening, tired and weary from the jolting of the ox-drawn wagon and the slow progress over the river roads to the prairie, the first thought was to mae camp at once. The more wary of our party pointed out that there were still some Indians in the country and decided it was best to camp in the open. At this time, there was scarcely any timber in the prairie, due to the fires which sprung up from the travelers' camps as they crossed the prairie to their future home farther west.

When we finally reached our destination, Waco, we crossed the Brazos River on the ferry boat in January of 1872. It was a severe winter when we reached Waco.

Miss Effie Cowan
n.d.

Mrs. Laura Hoover
Ozona, Crockett County

My husband, two children, and I left Kimble County when there were few roads even there, and none in the parts. We put our scant supplies and meager household goods in a covered wagon and started out on what was then a long and perilous journey.

Mr. Hoover and one cowboy drove 200 head of cattle and mapped out a road for me most of the way. When we started, he thought I could not manage the two babies, the team, and my rifle, so he hired a boy as teamster. I do believe that was the greenest boy I ever saw. He worried me all day long, and when we camped that first night and he got up next morning putting the horses' collars on backwards, I told my husband to send him back home before we got farther out on the road and we had him on our hands for all time. I could manage the team, the babies, and everything else better than I could him.

As I said, there were no roads after we got on out a ways,

and Mr. Hoover led on ahead and I followed, holding my baby on my lap, driving the team and snatching at Arthur every few minutes, as we bounced and jostled over hills and valleys.

We stretched a cowhide under the wagon as a cradle for the tired calves when they would give out. If one fell out, it was small bother to stop and restore him to his restful abode.

Somehow we escaped the Indian attacks of which we were in constant dread, and after camping along Devil's River for three months, looking for a suitable place to locate, we finally decided upon a place here in Crockett County.

Elizabeth Doyle
November 16, 1937

Mrs. W. M. Anderson
Durango, Falls County

When we went to Marlin, the county seat of our county [Falls], we crossed the river on a ferry boat. Sometimes when the river was low, people would wade across to save the fare of the ferry.

Miss Effie Cowan
n.d.

Mrs. Amelia Steward Christoffer
Mart, McLennan County

For public travel, there was a stage line in the early days from Old Springfield to Waco. The stop between Springfield and Waco was called "Midway," being midway between the two towns. This stage stop was located on the old Vickers farm, now known as the Corley farm. This was known as the old Waco and Springfield Road and passed between the Drinkard farm and our house.

The stage station was one big room made from cedar logs and would hold as many as six horses. They were kept there to change for fresh horses. The fresh horses were brought,

Chapter 3 — Frontier Travel

and by the time they were changed the driver would call "All ready" and away they went. The stage waited for no one; if anybody wanted to stop over, they took the next stage. If a traveler were taking a long trip, they often stopped at some town and waited for the next stage.

When we first came to Texas, stage travel was at its height of usefulness. There were several long routes for hundreds of miles, which reached the distant towns and military posts.

Very few railroads had been built, and the stage drivers, soon to be gone, were seeing their best days. They were heroes in their way, an important factor in the settling of the country.

There were many stories in those days of the different stage lines. One was of the Overland Trail, from Little Rock, Arkansas, through Texas and across the continent to California, which was marked along the way by rude stones bearing silent testimony of where some stage had been robbed and the driver killed. It was said that the driver was often killed by robbers or Indians as he slept with his gun in his hand, as he rested by the corral or in the rude stable where the horses were kept.

On some of the lines, there were the splendid "Concord Coaches," with four and six horses. Then the "dirt wagons" and "jerkies" in the less thickly settled routes. The stage driver in those days would have looked with contempt on the vehicles that now remain to supply remote places, untouched by a railroad or bus line.

But to return to our own little stage line, when it reached Waco it was a matter of great enjoyment to the people, old and young, to see it start on its return trip. The driver would mount his box (from where he drove) and gather the lines, and the agent and his helpers would hold the horses' heads while the travelers got on and the mail was being loaded. Then at a signal they would let go, and the driver would pull out in a dead run. The spirit of adventure was there the same as it is now in the air ship. Who knew but what the desperadoes would hold up the coach, or if it would reach its destination in safety from the Indians, floods, or robbers?

When we came to this part of the state, we came by wagon train from Texas City to our present home. The trip had a

Courtesy West Texas Collection, Angelo State University, San Angelo, Texas

Pony Express Stables.

wonderful interest to us. We never wearied of the life in the open air, which gave us such fine health. We had breakfast around three in the mornings, after which the wagons were ready with their occupants, the horses saddled for those riding, and at early dawn we were on the road. The beauty of the morning in this climate must be experienced to be realized. No fog as in the coast country, which hangs over the landscape, no wet grass to chill through and give you symptoms of rheumatism or ague, but the morning fresh and invigorating, as the sun bursts on the horizon in its blaze of glory, gives one the desire to be up and catch a glimpse of this beauty and a breath of the freshness of its pure air before the heat of the noon-day sun.

Close to the end of our journey up the fertile Navasota River country, the little city of Groesbeck was our last stop before we reached our destination, which was to be our future home, midway between Old Springfield and Waco. The country was rapidly recovering from the effect of the Reconstruction days, the after-effect of the War Between the States, and many new home seekers were coming to our part of the country. The advantages of soil and climate were being advertised throughout the old states, and many were seeking new fortunes here.

Miss Effie Cowan
n.d.

Mrs. Emily Kelly Davenport
Uvalde and Sabinal, Uvalde County

While we were engaged, myself and two other girls and our three boy friends, chaperoned by my married sister and her husband, took a trip to San Antonio that summer [1878]. We rode in two hacks drawn by horses, as there was no railroad west of San Antonio then. Our first night out, we stayed at Hondo with a friend. The boys spent the night in the hack and used the blankets and pillows we carried along. The rest of the party slept in the house. The next night found us in Castroville, and we secured rooms and a place to put the teams. We went then to see the Catholic church house which was practically new. It was a stone building, and beautifully decorated on the inside. I see that same church now when I pass through there going to San Antonio, and though it shows marks of age, it still serves the purpose for which it was intended. I think that church was the first to be built west of San Antonio.

The third night found us in San Antonio. We went out window-shopping, then took a ride on the street car which was drawn by a little Spanish mule. The little mule had a bell on its neck, which was a good signal that the street car was coming. He didn't have to pull the car all the time, as they had other mules stationed along the way so that they could put fresh ones to the car at different stops, and let the tired one rest. Sometimes the passengers would have to push to get the car started, if the car was heavily loaded.

We were out for a sight-seeing, so we went up to San Pedro Springs on the street car. The fare was cheap, but the travel was slow. I'll say, though, that the street car reached its destination safely. We were anxious to see the zoo that was out there. It was a pit dug about ten or twelve feet square and contained a bear, a wolf, and a coon. I don't remember any other animals, but they had just what we had seen all our lives, and we thought it was a splendid zoo. There were water fowls, such as ducks and geese, and a good collection of fish.

But mosquitoes! I couldn't sleep at all. There were no screens, of course, for we had never heard of anyone screening their houses then. Well, we made it through the night and was glad when it was over. We got up ready for more sight-seeing. We felt that we should spend one whole day in the city to make our trip more satisfactory. We were determined that we would visit an ice cream parlor and eat some ice cream. As for myself, I had never seen any ice cream in mid-summer. I had been having a slight toothache that day and was trying to forget it, but the first bite of ice cream I took, settled the fun with me till I went to the dentist.

We went to see the Government Tower that day. It wasn't finished, but it was the tallest building I had ever seen. We went straight up the stairway, then the steps began to wind. It looked too high for me and there was so much unfinished woodwork, that we decided to come down. We went over to Frost National Bank and then to Oppenheimer's store and a few other places, where we bought some new things for one of the girls who was going to get married later on.

It was just such a trip as this that my mother and father took to San Antonio after supplies once. It took five days to make a trip to San Antonio and back, and if it was muddy, it took a whole week. Well, they loaded up their wagon with the necessary supplies and they started home. My mother had bought a great assortment of dry goods. Of course, on the way back, it was a long trip and many an hour of just plodding along watching the road. Having to stop to cook meals

Chapter 3 — Frontier Travel

along the way and to let the team eat and rest, my mother wanted something to do. She hadn't brought her scissors along, but she hit on another plan of making a dress out of some of the material she had bought. Here is where another butcher knife came into play as a dressmaker's tool. She just cut out her dress with a sharp butcher knife and started to work on it and had the complete dress made by the time they got home.

Mrs. Florence Fenley Angermiller
March 14, 1938

Mrs. George C. Wolffarth
Estacado, Crosby County, and Lubbock, Lubbock County

My father, George M. Hunt, brought his family to the South Plains in 1884 from Sterling, Kansas. I was quite small then, but I have heard the details of the trip recounted numbers of times by my parents and the older children of our family.

There were fourteen people who started on this journey to the Texas Plains. They were Henry Baldwin and his family, Paul [Seely or Sealy ?], Miss Celia Corrigon, an elderly man whose name my father soon forgot, and then our family. We began the trip with three wagons, each drawn by two horses, and my father's buggy. Jimmie, our pet pony, was hitched to the buggy.

Now one of the wagons and the team belonged to the elderly man. My father had made a trade with him to bear his part of the expense of the trip if the man would bring a load of our household goods in his wagon, but on the [?] day out from Sterling, he changed his mind and would come no farther, so Father had to transfer mother's organ and the other things which the old man had been carrying on his freighter to the two remaining wagons, which were already overloaded, and we continued on our journey.

We began the long trip on the afternoon of the 5th of November and reached Estacado thirty-one days later, the 6th of December. Our route ran from Sterling to Dodge City, along the left bank of the Arkansas River.

At Dodge City the party turned south and took the Jones and Plummer Trail. We had three rivers to cross after that, before we reached our destination. First we crossed the Cimarron, which was treacherous on account of quicksand. There were accounts given of a whole outfit's having been swallowed up in the river bed a short time before this, and natives there advised our men to drive through the stream as quickly as they could, which they did, using the whips to keep the horses from stopping to drink, and we forded the river without disaster.

Next we came to the Canadian River. This river was not deep, excepting where holes had been washed out in the sand. A long train of wagons crossed just in front of us. These wagons were drawn by about twenty oxen. Men on horses rode across the river and picked out a crossing place before they let the ox-teams go in, so that we crossed behind them and had no trouble getting over to the other side.

When we reached Red River, we found it dry at this point and experienced no difficulty whatever in crossing it.

There were not many towns on our route. After we left Dodge City, the next town we reached was Mobeetie, then Clarendon. Two or three days after we left Clarendon, we came to the headquarters of the Quitaque Ranch. This ranch house was located near the mouth of Tule Canyon.

Our party had always traveled together, but on the second day after we left the Quitaque Ranch, my parents took my brother, little baby sister Myrtle, and me in the buggy and left camp at noon, before the wagons started. My father had been told that when we reached Blanco Canyon, we would have to go about two miles to reach Hank Smith's home, and he thought that we were only a few miles from Mr. Smith's place, but it was much farther than he had reckoned, and somehow he got confused and lost his way in the canyon. We were separated from the wagons and traveled around over trails through the canyon. Night found us in a ravine, far from our party, without food and water. The few wraps that my father and mother had brought along in the buggy were not sufficient to keep us warm. This was about the first week in December and it was rather cold in the canyon, even with

Chapter 3 — Frontier Travel

the mild weather that we had that winter. There was no moon and it was very dark. Father got out of the buggy and sought for a protected nook in the ravine where we could spend the night. Suddenly he came to a dugout. He crept inside where there was a faint light showing at the back of the dugout. This proved to be coals in a large fireplace at the back. There was a cottonwood back-log, partly burned. Father stirred the coals and soon had a fire going. No one appeared, and we spent the night alone in the dugout. There were no beds, but we were warm and in a measure protected from the wild animals that roamed the plains.

The greater part of the next morning was spent in trying to get back on the right trail, and at last the wagons were located and we were united again. After a good meal, we started out once more looking for the Smith house. We traveled all the afternoon without seeing a house anywhere. Night was coming down upon us and we were still in the canyon. Father and Mother debated whether to pitch the tent and make camp for the night or to go on. They always set up the stove and put up the tent for the night. The men got out and walked down the canyon a little way, trying to get their bearings, and then they heard the barking of dogs in the distance. We followed the sound and soon located Hank Smith's house. They were not surprised to see us, as Father had been sending his cousin, Dr. J. W. Hunt at Estacado, cards from different points of our journey, and Dr. Hunt had communicated with Mr. Smith, keeping him informed of our progress. The Smiths gave us a hearty welcome and we spent the night with them.

Ivey G. Warren
December 21, 1936

CHAPTER 4
Stories About Outlaws

Criminals mentioned in this chapter include John Wilkes Booth, Tom Ketchum, the James and the Younger boys, the Upshaws, Tom Cochran, and others.

Mrs. J. D. Rylee
Granbury, Hood County

John St. Helen, who may have been John Wilkes Booth, stayed with Mrs. Rylee's family in Somervell County for two years when she was a girl. She was born about 1858 and would have been about seven years old in 1865 when Abraham Lincoln was shot.

I was just a little girl at the time, but I remember when John St. Helen, the man who claimed he was John Wilkes Booth, the murderer of President Lincoln, came to our ranch in Somervell County. It was the first place he stopped when he got to that part of the country. He made a deal with my father for board and room, and stayed with us about two years. He always went by the name of St. Helen, and did not claim to be Booth until one time when he was sick and thought he was going to die. He confessed then to a lawyer, Finis Bates, that he was Booth. That was after he left our place.

He was well-educated and had fine manners, and he always wore the finest kind of clothes, broadcloth and linen and silk. We would get mail only about every two or three weeks, and he would get lots of mail each time, and some of it would be fine clothing, and we were sure, though we didn't know, that he got money through the mail.

When we and other people of the community would have parties and entertainments, we would get St. Helen to read for us, which he did wonderfully. He was always poised, and he seemed to know Shakespeare by heart.

I really believe he was Booth. My father would go to Dallas every two or three months with a big load of produce, and St. Helen went with him one time. St. Helen said later, after he had confessed to being Booth, that he was very much afraid while in Dallas that he would be recognized. Unless he were hiding out, it would seem strange for a man like him to be in a rough frontier country.

William V. Ervin
January 7, 1937

Mrs. Cicero Russell
San Angelo, Tom Green County

Tom Ketchum has eaten at our table many times. He wasn't as bad as he was said to be. I tell you, everything [everybody] in this country stole cattle. Even my father has stolen nice heifer calves, and nobody, even the big cattlemen, ate their own cattle. When they wanted beef, they found a fat beef animal belonging to somebody else.

Miss Nellie B. Cox
February 2, 1938

Mrs. Eleanor Ervin
San Angelo, Tom Green County

Mrs. Ervin lived at Uvalde, Knickerbocker, Sonora, and Ben Ficklin before moving to San Angelo in 1886. She lived at 216 E. 11th Street, San Angelo, at the time of this interview.

Tom Ketchum was a good boy. He got off with bad company. I knew all the boys. I heard Sam say that all he wanted was a horse branded SLS. I don't know why. Tom always did things for poor people, gave them what he could. Yes, he might have been a kind of Robin Hood.

I knew a girl in this country who joined up with a gang of desperadoes. When she was growing up, she was pert and different to most girls of that time, but she learned to shoot, first with one hand and then with the other hand. She helped her bunch in robberies and was finally caught, convicted, and sent to the "pen." She was real smart.

Miss Nellie B. Cox
n.d.

Mrs. Fayette Randal
Waco, McLennan County

When my mother was a young girl, the James and Younger boys, notorious desperadoes, camped for several days at the Sycamore Springs in the pasture near where Beulah Lane now runs. One night when the young people were having a party at the old home place, two of those outlaws walked in, with pistols and spurs on, and joined the other guests.

About 75 years ago [in the 1860s], a man named Lindsey was hanged by a mob in the ravine that is an extension of North Fifth Street, Waco, and so today that is known as Lindsey Hollow. He was hanged from an old crooked mountain cedar tree that grew on the left hand side of the road going north out of Waco. It leaned way out over the roadway.

Anne B. Hill
n.d.

Becky Sanford
San Angelo, Tom Green County

I remember a stage hold-up that took place about fifty-one years ago [about 1887]. We were living on Salt Creek between San Angelo and the present town of Miles. A young man who had lived around in the country, boarded at Jonathan Miles' and worked for Sol Schoonover, decided to turn robber.

Our house was on the main road and travelers frequently stopped for water. This young man, Andy, came by one day before noon, asked for water, and I told him as I told everybody, "Help yourself."

My husband was away from home, but when dinner time came, the fellow showed up and asked for dinner. I gave him what I had, and he offered me a five-dollar bill as pay. I didn't have any change and told him so. We watched him go over the hill and supposed that he had gone on his way, but that night at supper time here he was again. My husband was there by that time, and I told him that the same fellow had been there for dinner.

They sat down and ate, but passed things and did not say a word, one to the other. When they had finished eating, the stranger put down a silver dollar and said to me, "Well, I guess that will pay you for both meals."

That night he held up the stage not far up the road from our house. He pulled a sack over each man's head, tore out the cushions of the coach, and the women all screamed and cried. Sol Schoonover was a passenger, and the robber took Sol's gold watch and chain.

In those days the ladies wore "dusters," long coats generally made from linen, as protection from dust in traveling. One lady on this stage coach had made a pocket in the hem of her duster and had put her money in that, but when the robber showed up with his gun, this woman was so scared that she took her money out of her pocket and handed it over.

A posse of men and officers caught the robber the next day, and he was tried in court and sent to the "pen."

Miss Nellie B. Cox
February 10, 1938

Mrs. Laura Hoover
Ozona, Crockett County

I was helping my husband with the rounding-up and branding once, and we were out on the range together looking for a stray herd. All at once we rode right up on a very recently deserted camp fire. Shelled corn was scattered all about the camp, and the remains of a dead calf lay near by. It had been killed and the ribs removed and roasted. A short distance away lay a dead horse with a square of skin cut from his hip.

We had heard that the Ketchum and Upshaw outlaws were expected through, as they had robbed a train in another part of the country and were making their get-away through Crockett County. We were convinced that this was their camp and that the pack horse had been killed and the brand cut away. Later it was reported that they had buried the money there, also, and no longer needed the pack horse.

As we looked about, I says, "Now, Pap, they are bound to have friends somewhere in these parts, else this corn would not be here." This was long before there was an Ozona, but many years later in a Masonic Lodge in Ozona, a friend told my husband that my remark was overheard at that time, and he repeated to him the exact words I had said. This convinced Pap and me that someone was there in hiding as we explored the camp that day. They could have been either looking for or guarding the money; we never knew.

Elizabeth Doyle
November 16, 1937

Mrs. Frank Mitchell
Tascosa, Oldham County

Mrs. Mitchell, who came to Old Tascosa as a very young girl in 1884, knew Frank Valley, Fred Chilton, and Ed King, three cowboys who figured in the fatal shooting of March 21, 1886. She remembers them as nice young cowboys who treated her as considerately as any of the others and who acted as gentlemanly. Frank Valley was tall, dark, and handsome, an object of admiration of all the young girls, but considerably older than she. She, though very young, because of the scarcity of young girls, was permitted to go to dances as long as her father was about the place.

Chapter 4 — Stories About Outlaws

Jesse Sheets, the fourth of the men who died with their boots on, on the night of March 21, 1886, was a restaurant keeper who stuck his head out of the door to see what the shooting was all about and was accidentally shot.

She saw the four in the street the next morning, with their hats tipped over their faces.

Unidentified interviewer
March 25, 1938

Mrs. Mary Jane Ward
Glen Rose, Somervell County

When I came here [in 1870], Glen Rose was just a small place. People were scattered out around through the hills, living in log cabins; pole pens, we called them then.

There was not much farming, and there was some cattle raised. There was some whiskey-making going on all the time. This was a pretty rough place then.

There was one pretty bad sort of man here then. His name was Tom Cochran. He was born and raised in this country, and when he was a boy he went to work for a man on his ranch over in the edge of Bosque County. After a few years, Tom come back near here and had a herd of cattle himself. They said he branded all his boss's cattle he could with his own brand. Everybody branded all the cattle he could find, and nothing was ever done about it.

One time Tom Cochran caught eight or ten head of young cattle and branded them. He had a neighbor across the creek named McCamant. McCamant missed some of his cattle and went over and asked Cochran if he had seen any stray cattle. Cochran just laughed, and went and blurred his brand and put McCamant's brand on them and turned them back to McCamant. He didn't know he was branding his neighbor's cattle. That was all that was done about it.

My second husband, Mr. Ward, saw Tom Cochran kill a man in a billiard hall, but the first man Cochran killed was somewhere away out on the frontier in the West. He killed the man, thinking he had considerable money with him, but he just had a check. They say Cochran had a hard time cashing the check.

They kept the case in court about six years when he killed the man in Glen Rose, but they never done anything with him. They say he lured off or stole several girls; nothing ever seemed to be done with him about it.

William V. Ervin
n.d.

Mrs. George Fowler
Mart, McLennan County

The country was wild when we came to Mart [1875]. The country was all ranches, and there were plenty of cattle thieves to steal them. There were a few northern men who had come to Texas to buy the cheap land. Among them was Mr. Heaton, who for years owned the Heaton ranch across the Big Creek just south of us and directly west of the present town of Mart. Mr. Heaton was a young man and boarded with my father and mother. He wore a long black beard. After a few years, he returned to his native state and married, then he came back to the ranch and built a house where the ranch house had stood for many years. He had a daughter who married Captain Phillips of the U.S. Army. Mr. Heaton was killed; the wife and little daughter returned to their northern home, and the daughter married there.

A widow named Walker owned a ranch near Mr. Heaton. She had a son named Abner. This son had warned Mr. Heaton not to buy any of his mother's cattle, but Mr. Heaton ignored the warning and bought some of Mrs. Walker's cattle. Abner met Heaton when he came on Mrs. Walker's ranch to round up the cattle he had bought. Abner shot and killed Mr. Heaton instantly. Then Abner blacked up like a Negro and tried to make his escape. While crossing the old toll bridge at Waco, over the Brazos River, he passed a white boy who recognized Abner Walker's voice and reported to the officers. They gave chase, trailed Abner to Marlin and caught him. He was tried and sent to the penitentiary for ninety years, but was par-

Chapter 4 — Stories About Outlaws

doned after serving eighteen years.

When he came home, his hair had turned white, and hard labor caused him to walk with bent shoulders and bowed head like an old, old man. Owing to prejudice against northerners, Walker was received by friends and neighbors as though nothing had happened.

It was not an uncommon thing for cattle thieves to be hung when caught. The law was slow, and cattle-stealing was the greatest crime. One man was suspected of cattle-stealing for a long time. Finally, his guilt was proven and he was hung. No one knew or seemed to know who did the hanging. The man was named ___ ___. In those days, the men were their own law, and woe unto the ones found guilty of cattle theft.

Miss Effie Cowan
n.d.

Mrs. Mary Leakey Miles
Leakey, Real County,
and Uvalde, Uvalde County

[The town of Leakey was named for her father.]

We've entertained many an outlaw in our home. We didn't know who they were, for they came under different names, of course. A man named Longely stayed for awhile. He was a great desperado.

There were saloons there and some lively times in those days. Many a thing happened that weren't ever told.

Mrs. Florence Angermiller
October 25, 1937

Miss Mattie (Babe) Mather
San Angelo, Tom Green County

In the early days, Texas was somewhat made up of outlaws evading punishment in their own state. Their children would say, "What did your father do that he had to come to Texas?" Then they would relate murder and criminal stories that had brought their fathers to Texas.

>Ruby Mosley
>n.d.

CHAPTER 5
Kin to Texas Rangers

Mrs. Elizabeth Roe
Azle, Tarrant County

Elizabeth Roe's husband, Montgomery Roe, was a Texas Ranger. He was one of the group of Rangers who buried the bodies of the Cantrell women after they were hanged for cattle rustling.

I married Montgomery Roe in 1873, and a short time after we were married he enlisted in the Texas Rangers and served under Captain Willis Hunter. The company's headquarters were at Silver Creek.

After my husband enlisted, I again lived in fear. I knew the danger his work incurred. The rangers had to contend with cattle rustlers, fights between cattlemen and between ranchers and sheep men, and with desperadoes.

Those days the Rangers were called upon to do considerable burying. When some person's body was found, who had been shot or hanged, the Rangers were generally notified, and they buried the body. I saw my husband and a couple of fellow Rangers bury the Cantrell women, who were sometimes called by the name of Hill.

The Cantrell women were the leaders of a gang of cattle rustlers, and the rumor was that they were among the most troublesome rustlers in the state. The folks interested in the cattle business decided to stop these two women and hanged them to a tree near Springtown.

The Rangers would generally receive word that somebody discovered a person hanging to a limb of a tree or one that had been shot. As a rule, the report would be received a day or two after the incident happened. However, in the case of the Cantrell women, the report did not reach the Rangers until a couple of weeks or more after the hanging. When my husband's party went to get the bodies, they found the bodies on the ground, but their heads were still held by the noose of the rope. These bodies had remained until decay had caused the bodies to separate from the heads.

The Cantrell women were buried in a cemetery at Springtown. The graves were under a tree, and the Rangers tied the rope, with which the women were hanged, to a limb over the graves, as a marker for a rustler's grave.

My husband was mustered out of the Ranger service in 1875. We then made our livelihood by farming in the Ash Creek vicinity near what is now called Azle, Texas.

Sheldon D. Gauthier
n.d.

Mrs. George W. Jones
Waco, McLennan County

Mrs. Jones' father, a Texas Ranger, knew Bigfoot Wallace. She tells how Bigfoot got his name.

My father was born in Missouri. He came to Texas in 1846, when he was a boy about fifteen years old. It was under peculiar circumstances that my father came to Texas. His mother, my grandmother, had died, and grandfather married again. My father, whose name was David McFadden, was plowing in the field when his older brother, my Uncle John McFadden, came to my father and told him that grandfather had married again. My father didn't want grandfather to marry again—he didn't like the woman—so he just took the mule from the plow and got on it and started for Texas without even going back to the house. He fell in with a family, or group of people, who were coming to Texas, and they brought him along with him. They could see that he was just a boy, and I guess that

Chapter 5 — Kin to Texas Rangers

is why they took him along with them.

When they got to Texas, an army was being raised to fight Mexico, and my father joined it. He was large for his age, and so they let him join. He got down to Austin and San Antonio, but didn't get into Mexico.

After that war was over, he finally became a Texas Ranger and Indian fighter. He was with Bigfoot Wallace in the Indian fighting. He and Wallace and the men they were with were following a band of Indians in which was one with big feet. At least the white men often saw footprints in the trail of the Indians which were much bigger than the other footprints, and they thought it must be a big Indian which was making them.

At last they caught up with the Indians and had a fight with them and defeated them. During the fight, my father heard Wallace yelling, "I've got the bigfoot Indian!" When the fight was over, the men went and looked at Wallace's Indian, which Wallace had killed, and it was a big Indian with big feet. From that time on, the men called Wallace "Bigfoot". That is how Wallace came to be called Bigfoot, and not because his own feet were big, as lots of people think.

William V. Ervin
n.d.

CHAPTER 6
Civil War Stories

Mrs. Belle Little
Mart, McLennan County

Before my father [J.W. Mulloy] came to Texas, he freighted from Little Rock to Camden, Arkansas. He was a single young man and living at Atlanta, Arkansas, when the War Between the States was declared. He was twenty-one years of age. He enlisted under the Confederate Flag and served throughout the conflict under Generals [Nathan B.] Forrest and [John Bell] Hood of Texas.

I can remember how he told of their shoes wearing out and how they had to skin the hide from dead cattle to make moccasins to wear. When they returned to Georgia from the siege of Nashville, they would sing the songs of Texas while on the march, to relieve their homesick longing.

I can also remember how he told of how deeply he was affected when he surrendered his arms at Appomattox Court House, as he laid them down on the steps. On his return home, he took the responsibility of the support of a widowed mother and three young sisters. Father was a descendent of Pat Mulloy, who with his brother Jim came to America as stowaways on a ship from Ireland. This was before the Revolutionary War. They brought their possessions in a knapsack. They fought in the Revolutionary War.

Miss Effie Cowan
n.d.

Chapter 6 — Civil War Stories

Mrs. Lizzie Powers
Marlin, Falls County, and Mart, McLennan County

When the War Between the States broke out in 1861, my father [Dr. George Wyche] joined the Confederate Army and went as a surgeon. Some time after, his health failed and he was placed in the Post Office at Galveston, as I remember as Post Master. He served until the war closed. As a child, I can recollect hearing him tell of how sorely they needed medicine, such as morphine and whiskey, bandages and so on, for the soldiers; how they had to use hotels for hospitals, and when the wounded soldiers were brought in and they were out of bandages, they had to take the bed sheets and sterilize them to use in place of bandages.

I can also remember the stories of how the city of Galveston went wild with joy when the blockade was lifted, leaving them free to secure those supplies they needed; how they celebrated in honor of General [John B.] Magruder, both in Houston and Galveston, with banquets; how the Confederate soldiers, stationed at Galveston, were so royally treated by the residents since they had rescued them from this blockade and driven the Union soldiers out of the Bay.

Miss Effie Cowan
n.d.

Mrs. Ernestine Weiss Faudie
Indianola, Calhoun County, and Riesel, McLennan County

My father had two brothers to come with him from Germany and were in the Confederate army. Their names were August and Fritz Weiss. They were sent back home from the war on a furlough but had to return, and August was captured by the Yankees and taken prisoner and made to walk all the way to the prison. He was later exchanged and came home. The other brother, Fritz, came home after the war was over and took tuberculosis and died from this, which he contracted in the army.

When any of the soldiers on either side came through our place, they took anything they could find. The rebels felt that they had a right to it for they were fighting for us. They took our horses and killed our hogs and cows to eat and took our corn. When the blockade was on and we could not get coffee, we made it out of sweet potatoes. We cut them up and dried them and boiled them and drank this for coffee.

And speaking of the soldiers, I remember an incident that is amusing now, but at the time to the neighbor it was anything but amusing. When a group of soldiers passed this neighbor's, she tied a hog to the bed post so they would not see it, but they stopped for a drink of water and heard the hog grunting and so came into the room and took the hog and barbecued it out in the yard, and ate it before the neighbor's very eyes.

Miss Effie Cowan
n.d.

Mrs. Annie Shaw
Mart, McLennan County,
and San Antonio, Bexar County

I was born on the 29th day of October, 1870, near Griffin, Georgia. I was one of seven children by my father's second wife. Their names were William and Elizabeth Woodward. As I was born at the close of the days of Reconstruction, I can remember many things that were handed down to me by my parents, of those days and the days of the Civil War.

When the war broke out, the communities selected one of their men to stay and look after the women and children. He was in charge of the business of those who had no man in the family left, and my father was the one selected for our little community. They were within nine miles of Sherman's March to the Sea, and his soldiers spread out in detachments, and our community suffered from their raids in the loss of livestock and feedstuff. So far as I can remember, they did not

Chapter 6 — Civil War Stories

burn or destroy the homes, but the women were insulted and force was used if they tried to prevent the taking of the provisions. They were forced to keep the soldiers in their homes and cook for them when they passed through the community.

My two uncles on my mother's side were soldiers in the Confederate Army. I can remember hearing my mother tell about how they were stationed at one time near our home, and the women of the community would go to the camp and take their boys clothing and food. My uncles' names were William and Millage Hartsfield. Uncle Will Hartsfield was the father of Mrs. J. W. Howard of Mart. He returned from the war, and about the year 1875 he moved to Texas and settled in Milam County, near the town of Calvert, where he reared his family, and two of his sons are still living in this county.

My parents were still in Georgia during the days of Reconstruction. Father passed away when I was three years old, but I remember many things my mother told me of those days. The men who were sent from the North to hold the main offices were called carpet-baggers. Many of them were unprincipled and profiteered off the whites. They placed the Negroes in the offices over the whites, as history shows, and the white people underwent many humiliating things at the Negroes' hands during those days. One of the most humiliating things they had to bear was the insults from the Negro guards who were stationed along the highways and entrances to the towns. If they spoke to a woman, the woman dared not reply.

The most appealing thing to my heart, that she told me, was how the slaves stayed and helped to take care of the family and the crops while the masters were gone to the war. Especially do I remember old Aunt Harriet, who had helped to care for us children. When we left, the neighbors came in to bid us good-bye. They were lined up in a row, and the family marched by and shook hands with each one of the friends to bid them farewell. Aunt Harriet stood at the end of the row, with her handkerchief in her hands and a red bandana on her head, and she wiped away the tears which were streaming down her face, as she bade each one of us good-bye. She has long since gone to her heavenly home. I can also remember her lullabies, as she sang us to sleep in our childhood; and when our mother needed us to be kept quiet, it was always Aunt Harriet who could hold us spellbound as she told us the Negro folk and fairy tales. The ghost stories were our special delight. Aunt Harriet would come up to "the big house" to sit with my mother on a Sunday afternoon and talk and have my mother read the Bible to her.

It was a hard thing for us to leave that dear old country, but the new state of Texas was calling to the ones who were interested in founding new homes where the land was plentiful and cheap.

Miss Effie Cowan
n.d.

Courtesy West Texas Collection, Angelo State University, San Angelo, Texas

Women's hat styles in the 1890s.

CHAPTER 7
Indian Stories

Mrs. Elizabeth Roe
Azle, Tarrant County

Mrs. Roe was born at Ash Creek settlement, three miles west of Azle, January 6, 1855.

    Our most feared trouble was the Indians. They were a constant menace. In the vicinity of the Ash Creek settlement there were frequent Indian raids, and a number of settlers were killed during my childhood days. Also, a number of women and children were kidnapped.

    My mother's home was raided several times, but the good Lord was with us. We were never injured, but did lose horses and food.

    I recall one night when mother was away at our neighbor, Bedwell's, place, where there was sickness at the time. Brother and I were sitting up waiting for mother to return home. Suddenly, we heard a noise similar to an owl's screech. Brother said, "Listen to the owls screeching."

    "It sounds like owls, but it's not," I replied.

    "It's Indians, I bet," he suggested. "Let's hide."

    From the time we were old enough to have any understanding of the meaning of words, mother had dinned in our ears to evade Indians, and when old enough to handle a gun she taught us to shoot. We had two hiding places: One in the loft of the cabin and one in a hole under a rock located in a brush patch near the cabin.

When we heard the owl's screech, we blew out the candle and crawled to the hole under the rock. We were not there long when Indians appeared, mounted on ponies, and rode up to the house. They scrutinized the place, then went to the corral and took two of our most valuable horses.

Indian scares would happen frequently, because of reports that Indians were seen in the surrounding territory. On these occasions, everyone would live in fear until word was received that the Indians had moved on. Frequently, we have remained in the woods hiding for two or three days at a time, when word was passed around that Indians were depredating somewhere in the surrounding country. During my childhood days, we lived more or less in constant fear of Indian raids.

While we Fletchers were not kidnapped by the Indians, there were several people in the vicinity who were carried off and some killed by the Indians. Among those to meet with this misfortune were the Davis and the Hamilton families.

The Davis family lived on Walnut Creek. The members of this family were killed and carried off. I don't recall of hearing that any of the Davis folks were ever heard of after the raid. The Hamilton family, which also lived on Walnut Creek, were raided. The parents were killed and two children were carried off. One child was sick at the time, and after it was carried for some distance the Indians rolled the child in a blanket and laid it on the ground in some brush. The child, of course, cried. After riding for a distance away from the child, the Indians returned and killed it. It was supposed they feared the cry would attract attention.

One of the Hamilton boys was away from home at the time of the raid. He set out to find and retake his sisters. It was about a year later when he located a sister. He traded for the child and then learned about the killing of the other child.

The conditions which I have related were what we lived under until I reached womanhood.

Sheldon F. Gauthier
n.d.

Chapter 7 — Indian Stories

Mrs. George W. Jones
Waco, McLennan County

I was born in McLennan County in 1860, and have lived in the county all my life. While we were living about twenty miles from Waco, on Hog Creek, my father [David McFadden] captured the last Indian in this part of the country. It was long after the Indians had quit making raids down this far, although they still raided and stole horses and killed settlers in Comanche, Hamilton, and Brown counties. I always had a horror then, when I was a little girl of those counties, because of the stories of Indian depredations we would hear then, and I still don't feel any desire to go to those counties.

It was about 1865 when my father caught the Indian. One cold, moonlight night my father went out to the corral to turn loose some horses, and when he opened the gate they all ran out but one horse, and it stood near the barn with its head and neck in the shadow of the barn. He thought it was one of his horses, and wondered why it didn't run out with the others. He went up to it and put his hand on its neck and ran his hand up along the neck toward the head, and felt a rope around the pony's neck. He ran his hand along the rope and touched the Indian, and the Indian yelled, "Indian! Comanche!" My father saw him then, as the Indian was standing in the shadow of the barn. My father grabbed him, but the Indian didn't make any resistance. My father searched him, and didn't find anything on him in the way of a weapon, not even a pocket knife. Father brought the Indian into the house. He was a young Indian, and he was cold and about half-starved. My father tried to talk to him in some Indian language he knew, but the Indian couldn't understand. All he could do was point to the west and indicate he came from that way.

My father wanted to go and get the neighbors and all take council and see what ought to be done, as my father thought there might be other Indians around who would attack the settlement, but my mother and my older sister and myself were scared to death, and we wouldn't let him stick his nose out of the house. I was just a little thing, about five years old, but I was sure scared. We made Father wait until morning to

A Legacy of Words — Texas Women's Stories 1850-1920

Courtesy West Texas Collection, Angelo State University, San Angelo, Texas

Unidentified army medical officer and children, 1885.

Chapter 7 — Indian Stories

go to the neighbors'. We gave the Indian something to eat, and he ate plenty. My father spread some quilts and blankets down before the fireplace, and let the Indian sleep there, and my father slept on a bed in the same room, and he said he didn't think the Indian moved from the time we went to sleep until he woke up the next morning.

The next morning father called the neighbors in, and they were afraid there were other Indians around, but they hadn't seen any, and the Indian that Father had caught said he was the only one. They couldn't get much out of him but that, and that he came from the west. They had no idea what he was doing there except that he had got lost from a raiding party in the country farther west and had wandered down into our part of the country. We never did know for sure where he came from, and he was always a mystery to us.

One of the men who came to our home that morning said he would take the Indian to his place and take care of him to work for him, and the Indian went with him, but he left the man after two or three years because the man wasn't kind to him. That was the last wild Indian ever seen or heard of in this country.

My father was in the Dove Creek fight, and marched from Waco with some of the Indian fighters. One night they marched all night. It was very cold weather and there was snow on the ground, and the men suffered a lot from the cold, especially the wounded.

My father settled here when there was hardly any Waco here, and lived in this county the rest of his life. I knew Neil McLennan, the man for whom the county was named. He was one of the finest men I ever knew.

William V. Ervin
n.d.

Mrs. Belle Little
Mart, McLennan County

Some of my earliest memories are of the continual fear of the Indians. While we were living at Comanche, Texas, they still roved over the country stealing cattle, horses and food and feedstuff, as they were too lazy to work and would slip away from the Indian Reservation and prey on the settlements.

One day (I was only a small child then) while at church at Comanche, a rider came and warned the congregation that there was smoke from the Indian camps, and the meeting broke up while the congregation fled to their homes, but this attack did not materialize as the band drifted in another direction. But to this day I can remember the feeling of fear we had.

Miss Effie Cowan
n.d.

Mrs. J. A. Kemp
Wichita Falls, Wichita County

Quanah Parker was a friend of Mrs. Kemp's brother. Most of the experiences with Indians that Mrs. Kemp speaks of here were related to her husband's owning a dry goods and grocery store in Wichita Falls, where he "did a big business with the Indians."

The Indians and the cowboys kept me alive. There was always something interesting going on. Mr. Kemp did a big business with the Indians, and it was very interesting to me just to go down to the store and watch them. I had long red hair which I wore braided and wound around my head. One day Mr. Kemp's brother-in-law touched my braids and called the Indians' attention to it. One of them looked very earnest and pointed heavenward. It seemed that their idea of their god was a large man with flowing red hair. Some of the squaws came up and were feeling of my hairpins; I took one and gave it to her and said, "Yours," and motioned to her to put it in her hair, and she got out her knife to cut it off.

At the back of the store Mr. Kemp had a bone yard. The Indians gathered up the dried bones of cattle, buffalo, etc., and brought them to trade for groceries and dry goods. The

Chapter 7 — Indian Stories

warriors came riding on ahead and the squaws followed on wagons with the bones. The Indian men sat against the house and smoked while the squaws unloaded the bones. Mr. Kemp kept the bones until he had a carload and then shipped them to the East for fertilizer, etc.

One day in warm weather I was at the store when the squaws came in very hot and worn out from unloading bones. They always wore those big heavy shawls no matter how hot it got. I pointed to them and said, "Hot," then I picked up a piece of red table cloth and put it around my own shoulders and said, "Cool." I pinned it on with safety pins. They had their blankets pinned on with mesquite thorns. Then I started selling red tablecloths.

We sold all we had, and Ward and Stanley sold all they had. You never had to tell more than one; they passed the word around. They were delighted with the safety pins; they had never seen any before.

They didn't know how to count money; about all they could say was, "two-bats," meaning two-bits, or 25 cents. They would sell you a big fish for a quarter, or a turkey weighing twelve or fifteen pounds for the same amount.

Mr. Kemp also opened up a store at Harrold, Texas, which was the terminus for the Fort Worth and Denver for a long time. One time I went up to Harrold with Mr. Kemp. Quanah Parker was there with two of his wives and some of his children. I took a little pink chambray dress of my baby's and dressed his baby up in it. He was delighted; he asked my baby's name and when I told him, "Syble," he pointed to his baby and said, "Syble." He named his baby after mine (Mrs. Newton Mayer).

My brother, Arch Anderson, and Quanah Parker were very good friends. Quanah Parker had one son that was a preacher. He was here a few years ago and put on a war dance at the Women's Forum.

Ethel C. Dulaney
n.d.

Mrs. Helen Ketchum
San Angelo, Tom Green County

Mrs. Helen Ketchum, wife of the late J. Van Ketchum, tells of Jim Ketchum (Van's father) being killed by the Indians. Eugene McCrohan, one of the early settlers of this country, gave the details of the story to Mrs. Ketchum. Jim Ketchum was a cousin of Tom Ketchum, the noted outlaw. This introduction and the following account were written by the interviewer, Nellie B. Cox.

In the spring of 1867, Jim Ketchum started with a large herd of cattle to Fort Sumner, New Mexico. The government had seven thousand Navajo Indians imprisoned at Fort Sumner, and the range country supplied the beef for the prisoners.

Other herds gradually joined that of Ketchum, two of those known being Eugene McCrohan and Sam Gholson. They traveled slowly, reaching the Hondo River in New Mexico that fall, and finding plenty of water and grass, wintered there with their herds. This camp was about where Roswell now stands. They had no Indian trouble, although there were lots of Indians. A troop of cavalry was stationed at Camp Charlotte at the head of Kiowa Creek.

Having sold the cattle for a satisfactory price, these men prepared to return to their homes. Ketchum and two companions traveled "light" carrying their supplies on pack horses. They left before the others were ready. Mr. McCrohan purchased two Santa Fe or Murphey wagons, as they were known in those days, and to each of these wagons were hitched three yoke of oxen. Thus, they proceeded on their slow and tedious journey, but always kept within three or four days' travel of Mr. Ketchum.

One morning one of their party was sent out to kill a buffalo. In a short time he came rushing back to the wagons yelling, "Indians! Indians!" but on being questioned, admitted that he had not seen any Indians but had found the body of a man riddled with bullets. Several men of the party went to investigate, finding the bodies of Ketchum and his two companions, a McDonald boy, and a Mr. Comperry, near what was called the Mustang Waterhole. One of the men rode rapidly to Camp Charlotte with the news, and a detachment of cavalry was sent to the scene. The bodies of the men were buried by the soldiers, near the present day town of Tankersley. The graves are still recognizable.

The ground and surroundings at the scene of the fight gave evidence that the three men put up a gallant fight. They took refuge in a small arroyo where they were well protected on three sides. On the open side stood a hackberry tree, and the Indians took advantage of the protection afforded by the tree. So fierce was the gun fire that the tree was cut down. How long the battle lasted will never be known, but the ground was covered with shells. Mr. Ketchum and his companions had a good supply of ammunition, fine guns, and there were never braver men than those behind the guns.

After the men were killed, the Indians had thrown rocks until the bodies were almost covered. The "greenbacks" with which Mr. Ketchum had been paid for his cattle, were torn in pieces and scattered over the ground, the Indians evidently not realizing its value. The fragments of paper money were gathered up and brought to Mrs. Ketchum who sent them to the United States Treasury for redemption.

Miss Nellie B. Cox
n.d.

Mrs. Cicero Russell
San Angelo, Tom Green County

My father, John Burleson, came from Alabama to the San Saba country. There he accumulated a small bunch of cattle, and then for some reason he went to Williamson County. There he married my mother, Katy Williams.

Grandfather Williams had been killed by the Indians before the Civil War. He and a man by the name of Freeman had started a herd of cattle to New Mexico. After arming all their men and mounting them on good horses, it left Grandfather and Freeman unarmed and grandfather riding a mule. After they got the cattle strung out and driving well on the trail, Grandfather and Freeman started back home intending to get other horses and guns. On the way home in the late afternoon, Freemen got off his horse to go down to a spring for a drink of water. The Indians evidently surrounded him. Grandfather tried to go to his aid but both were hacked to pieces by tomahawks. These Indians were trailing the herd of cattle, but when they tried to stampede the herd, the cowboys drove them off.

My mother used to tell that when she was a small child, Indians would prowl around at night. They would whistle through a crack by the chimney and would shake the door. All the children would be quiet, hardly breathe, and Grandmother would have the fire covered, and the Indians would go away.

My mother's brother had a paint pony which they kept in a log crib and then chained to a stout log so it wouldn't be so easy for the Indians to get him. Grandmother would often give the Indians corn bread and they liked it.

Mother told of another time in Brown County that Grandfather, his brother, a man named Mosley, and Father were working cattle away from home. The Indians came around the house in the brush and called like coyotes and owls. There didn't seem to be many of them, but this time Mother got ready. She took an old musket, put in everything like bolts she could find and tamped them down. She sat waiting all night but the Indians didn't show up.

The next day, however, they surrounded Father and the other men, and in the fight, Father received two slight wounds. The Indians got the horses but long years after, Father was paid for them. We called it "entering Indian claim" when we sent in the number of horses stolen.

Father took that gun mother had loaded, tied it up in the fork of a tree, with a long wire to the trigger. When he pulled the wire, the whole gun exploded. He said that would surely have killed something.

Another time at night, Mother heard an unusual noise outside. It sounded to her like it might be Indians sharpening their knives or rubbing them together. This kept up for a long time, then everything was quiet. The next morning, there were two deer (bucks) with their horns locked together in the small clear space in front of the house.

My family moved to this country in 1875. We lived just below the town of Ben Ficklin. We ran a dairy for awhile. While we had the dairy, a man by the name of Taylor worked for us. He had been taken by the Indians when he was a baby about two years old and had lived with the Indians until he was nine or ten. He never wanted to live with his people, always said that the Indians had been good to him, that they lived happier then the whites and even as a grown man his one idea was to live with the Indians again.

Miss Nellie B. Cox
February 2, 1938

Mrs. J. D. Rylee
Granbury, Hood County

My father and mother lived in Alabama when they were married, and their fathers each gave them 25 slaves, and they came to Texas in the early fifties. They settled on Paluxy Creek, not far from Glen Rose, which was then known as Barnard's Mill, but there was no town there at that time. That was then Johnson County, then Hood county, then Somervell County. We lived in three counties without moving. I was born there 78 years ago. My father's name was William McDonald.

The Indians were bad then. My father required us all to be in the house before dark, and we didn't have a window so that a light could show through it. My father raised fine horses, the steeldust mostly, and the Indians sure liked to get hold of them. They stole a good many horses from my father. They usually came on moonlit nights.

My father was a member of the Ranger force organized to fight the Indians. He was wounded three times by them. Once an arrow struck him just above his forehead and went back over his head, but his hat saved him from a bad hurt. Another time an arrow clipped through the skin of his throat.

Another wound was when an arrow took off the thumb of his hand in which he was holding his pistol, firing at the Indians.

The Caddo Indians were friendly, and would help the white people with their work. They would take their pay in farm produce, but they wanted mostly milk, butter, and eggs. They would come to our place and sit in a row with their cups to get sweet milk. My father would have one of the Negroes take a large bucket of milk and pour each Indian a cupful of milk. They would say, "Me good Indian. Me no hurty you." I was very much afraid of them, anyway.

They would steal, though. I don't think I ever saw an Indian that wouldn't steal whatever he could. A band of them camped for some time on the creek now known as Squaw Creek, and it got its name from them.

My father and other men of the community had been trying to decide on a suitable name for the creek when two men came there from the Indian reservation in Oklahoma to see these Indians about going there. They went to the camp of the Indians on the creek, but each time they went they found only two or three old men and a bunch of squaws and children. The men of the Caddos, who were able, were gone on a stealing expedition, and they would be gone sometimes several weeks, and when they would come back they would bring plenty of stuff. The men who wanted to see the Indian men told my father they would like to suggest a name for the creek. They said to name it Squaw Creek on account of the squaws camped on it, and the settlers agreed to call it that.

The Comanches made a raid and carried off the wife and three little children of a doctor named Box who lived in our part of the country. Two of the children were girls, three and five years old, and the other was a baby. The Indians tied the mother on a wild horse which tried to throw her off, and they made her carry the baby, which cried, and she couldn't get it to stop. The Indians didn't like that, so one of them grabbed the baby and smashed its head against a tree. They took the mother and two girls to their camp near San Angelo.

The white people got together and followed them. Charles Barnard was with them, and they decided that he would try to ransom the woman and children. He had been in this country for several years and had trapped for furs over it and

Chapter 7 — Indian Stories

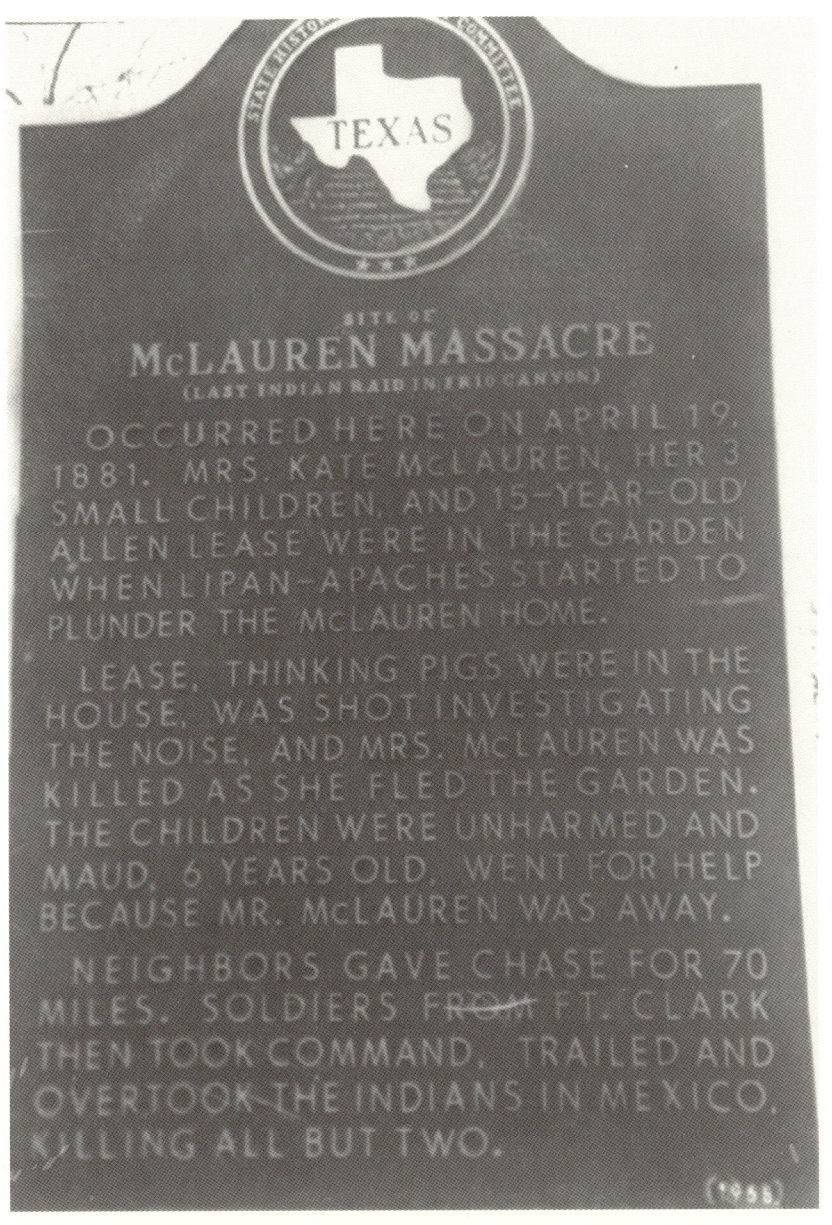

Courtesy Southwest Collection, Texas Tech University, Lubbock, Texas

Historical marker at the site of the McLauren Massacre (last Indian raid in Frio Canyon).

was well known to the Indians, and they were friendly with him. He would trade them goods for their furs. The men of the rescue party stayed away from the Indians' camp while Barnard went to talk with the Indians. They would not hear of giving up the woman and her children, at first. Before the posse got there, they had tortured the children by burning their feet until their feet were drawn up in a knot, and stayed that way. The little girls grew up and were grown young ladies with club feet.

Barnard talked to the Indians a long time, and at last got them to agree to give up the captives, but he had to give them a great deal to get them to do it. Nobody else but him could have got them to do it.

Barnard was a smart businessman, and he knew how to get along with the Indians and make them like him. His wife was a Spanish girl named Juana Cavassoo. She and a cousin of hers were captured by the Indians when they were eight or nine years old, and Mrs. Barnard was kept by them until she was old enough to be married, and was ransomed by Charlie Barnard and his brother. It took the Barnards several months to get the Indians to agree to let them have her.

Mrs. Barnard said the Indian girls abused her and her cousin. Mrs. Barnard said she fought the Indian girl who started mistreating her and her cousin, and knocked the Indian girl down and choked and beat her and tried to kill her. Her cousin, Mrs. Barnard said, was timid and would not fight the Indian girls. The Indians were proud of Mrs. Barnard's spirit, and the chief took her under his care and saw that she was treated right. But they tied her cousin to a tree and burned her to death. Mrs. Barnard tried to get the Indians to spare her cousin.

My brother, Jack McDonald, was in the fight about 1872, when a band of seven Indians were cornered in Robinson Creek and all of them killed. It was the rule among the settlers that when the Indians made a raid, for each person whose home was on the route the white men were taking to follow the Indians, to have horses ready to re-mount the men. My brother got to that Indian fight that way. The Indians while on their raid had been to one place where there was a washing on the line, and when the Indians were found they were dressed in the clothes and wrapped in the bed sheets. They got down in the creek under the bank and behind a log or fallen tree and brush in such a way that the white men couldn't get in position to shoot at the Indians without exposing themselves. One man was killed and another one badly wounded trying to get shots at the Indians, who were armed with bows and arrows. A rain came up and got the Indians' bowstrings so wet they wouldn't shoot, and so the settlers killed all the Indians. The bowstrings were made of rawhide.

There were six Indian men and one squaw, but she was dressed in such a way that the white men couldn't tell but what she was a man until they had killed the Indians. They don't know which one of the men killed her. One of the older men told my brother that he could have the woman's scalp if he wanted it. My brother got it and brought it home, though the hair was so full of "nits" it looked speckled.

I remember when I was fourteen, six couples of us, six boys and six girls, rode up on Comanche Peak to have a picnic. We were all armed with pistols, rifles, and knives to fight Indians in case they bothered us, but I don't think there was much danger, as they had been about all driven out of the country by then. I guess our folks wouldn't have let us gone if they had thought there was much danger. We did a lot of shooting and had a big time.

William V. Ervin
January 7, 1937

Mrs. Mary Leakey Miles
Leakey, Real County, and Uvalde, Uvalde County

My father run stock, and his oldest boy was riding with him when he was so little my father had to tie him on the horse. He did this, a whole lot, on account of Indians.

We've seen Indians on the mountains around our home. Once my brother and my sister just older than me started up on the mountain one evening. My brother was ahead of us and pretty soon he whistled and we knowed to stop, so we did. My brother broke to run, and then we knew there were Indians. We got back home safe but the Indians took a lot of stock that night.

My father was shot to pieces by the Indians once when he was visiting Mr. [Anglinis?] folks over in Sabinal. He and my mother had gone to spend the day over there. The Indians had come to the corral to steal horses and were run off, so my father and six or seven men went upon the mountain to trail them, and he got to the top and waved back for the others to come on up when the Indians shot him. He jumped off of a high bluff when he saw they had him, and he fell from bush to bush, catching his way as he went down. They thought he was dead, of course, and the Indians were slipping up on him to scalp him when he grabbed his six-shooter and begun cursing them.

He was an awful person to curse, and that's how the white men knew where he was and got to him, they heard him cursing. The Indians run but they didn't know the gun was empty. At least, my father thought it was. He had another shell and didn't know it.

Mrs. Florence Angermiller
October 25, 1937

Mrs. Emma Kelly Davenport
Sabinal and Uvalde, Uvalde County

Indians had to be taken into consideration at this time, because they were constantly coming into the settlements and robbing and stealing. My father had narrowly missed being ambushed by them more than once. He decided that it would be safer to leave his family at Uvalde, even though it was only a village, for there were soldiers down at Fort Inge, and it was far better protection against the Indians.

When cool weather came along, mother wanted to go back

Chapter 7 — Indian Stories

to kill her hogs up on the ranch and put up her meat and lard. Mrs. Thompson decided to go along, too, for she had moved to Uvalde to live while Mr. Thompson was gone, the same as we had. They got two neighbor boys to go along horseback, and they put all us children in the wagon and we started out.

We had gone about forty miles up in the canyons, and when we reached Nolton Creek on Uvalde Prairie, we noticed a mounted Indian leading another horse. I remember that the horse he was leading seemed a little crippled, and I think he tied him and stopped to try to make out what we were doing, or how many men there were. My mother told my two oldest brothers to get out and get two long sticks and get on the horses that were hitched to the wagon. They did so, and then she told the two boys that were on horseback to tie their lariats to the tongue of the wagon and start out. She had all of us children sit up in the wagon with hats on to make us look like men or big boys.

Mrs. Thompson was frightened and was afraid that we were all going to be killed, but my mother told her to have faith in the Lord and all would be well. She was a courageous woman and one of the calmest and most serene persons I ever knew. She wasn't easy to get ruffled. Her scheme worked like magic, because the Indian couldn't tell for sure how many men there were, for it looked like there were four mounted men, armed with guns. Indians knew that men with rifles could do business in those days.

Even after my father got back to Texas, the Indians were still pilfering and stealing horses. He was taking us across the country one time from Uvalde to the ranch, and we stopped at one of our places at the Blue Water Hole for the night. There was a house there, and we were going to spend the night there before going on in home. We unloaded the wagon and went into the house, and my father turned the horses loose, and they hardly got ten steps before the Indians had them. We didn't know it until next morning, but we saw by the tracks what had happened. My father had to walk about ten miles to get another team to take us on up to our home.

Mrs. Florence Angermiller
March 14, 1938

Mrs. Lizzie Powers
Marlin, Falls County,
and Mart, McLennan County

I will tell you about this fight [the Indian fight that followed the Marlin-Morgan Massacre] as it has been handed down through the times to us, from the other two brothers who were also in this fight.

In the excitement of the battle, Jackson was wounded and fell off his horse. His brothers and companions stopped and tried to put him back on the horse. The horse was so frightened that he plunged, so they could not get him on the horse. He told them that he knew he was killed and for them to leave him and save themselves, before they, too, were killed. The two brothers were William and Lewis who were in this fight, and the story has been handed down by them. Jackson was killed, but his self-sacrifice for his companions will live as long as there is a Powers left to tell the story.

This fight was between the settlers and the Indians, on the highway between Waco and Marlin, ten days after the Morgan-Marlin Massacre. The whites were led by Captain Benjamin Bryan of Bryan's Station, and the noted Indian chief, Jose Maria, led the Indians. This fight occurred in 1839.

Miss Effie Cowan
n.d.

CHAPTER 8
Hardships

Elizabeth Roe tells how her mother managed as a widow; Mattie (Babe) Mather was blind; Laura Hoover lived a long way from a doctor, saw few women, and had to cope with everything, including rattlesnakes, when her husband was away; and Mrs. J.D. Rylee talks about wild cattle and hogs.

Mrs. Elizabeth Roe
Azle, Tarrant County

Elizabeth Roe was born at the Ash Creek settlement, near Azle, January 6, 1855. Her mother was widowed when Elizabeth's father died while in the Confederate Army. Elizabeth tells how her mother coped, with three children to raise alone and a small farm to manage.

My home was a one-room log cabin, similar to the homes of all other settlers. The settlers in the Ash Creek district built their homes from logs. The only difference in these structures was the number of rooms each contained. Some of the cabins contained two rooms. These cabins were all built by hand. The lumber was hand-made and, by hand, worked into doors, window frames, and flooring.

Our living was obtained from the patch of ground which we cultivated and planted to foodstuff and cotton. Also, from cattle which ranged in the territory and wild game that abounded in the woods.

My father enlisted in the Confederate Army when the Civil War started, and became ill and died while serving in Virginia. This event left mother alone to rear her children. My mother and us children attended to the farm work. I was the oldest, with a brother a year younger, and a baby brother constituted the family of children. While we worked hard and had many difficulties to contend with, we always had sufficient food and an ample supply of clothing.

We raised a little wheat and corn. From these grains we secured our flour and corn meal. We paid out no money for grinding our grain. A portion was taken by the miller in payment for his grinding charge. We had a vegetable garden, had a few chickens, and a couple of milk cows which were pastured for our butter and milk supply.

The material for our clothing was raised by us, and from this material we made the cloth and the clothes. The material was cotton, and wool from the sheep we raised.

As a child, with my brothers, I spent many nights helping mother pick cotton seeds, carding cotton, wool, and assisting her to spin the material. The weaving of the materials into thread with the spinning wheel was the next process after carding, and the old spinning wheel could be heard many nights into the late hours. After spinning came the weaving process on the hand loom, then the dyeing process. The dyes were made from bark and other vegetable matter.

When we completed a suit or dress and succeeded in producing a nice color shade, we were mighty proud of our garments.

The clothes we made and sat up nights to produce by a tedious hand method gave me more satisfaction than any factory-produced garment I have ever worn. Well might we be proud of our garments those days, because our very soul was put into the making of our clothes. Many, many, nights my mother and the children sat working at the loom or spinning wheel till our eyelids would refuse to remain open, and we would be forced to quit work.

Our patch of cultivated ground was fenced with a split rail fence. This was necessary to prevent cattle from molesting our crop. Also, to keep out deer and other wild animals, which would destroy the grain.

We raised a few cattle, which ran in the creek bottoms. We followed the custom of the day and branded our stock and let the animals find their own living.

From our cattle we secured our beef, and sold a few head for money that was necessary for the few articles we had to buy. Also we had a herd of hogs, which found their own living, with the exception of a small amount of corn which we fed for the purpose of keeping the animals close to our farm. This herd of hogs supplied our hog meat and lard.

Besides the domestic animals, the woods were full of various kinds of game, such as deer, wild turkey, partridge, and many other edible wild animals. Because of this supply of domestic and wild animal meat, we were able to pick our choice of preferred cuts. In addition, besides our own cattle, there were hundreds of other cattle in the bottoms, which drifted in from the cattle ranches. In those days it was not considered wrong to take a yearling for meat supply, even if its brand was that of someone else.

Sheldon F. Gauthier
n.d.

Miss Mattie (Babe) Mather
San Angelo, Tom Green County

When I was a little school girl eleven years of age, paralysis struck an optic nerve which caused me to be blind. I suffered and worried until we found that I could continue my education by entering the Institute for the Blind, at Austin, Texas. I entered this institute in 1873 and received my diploma in 1881. I remained there a year longer continuing my music, which proved to be helpful and entertaining throughout these many years.

In October, 1900, I came to San Angelo. My sister and brother kept insisting that I come out and claim some school land by paying a small fee. Guides were located in San Angelo; as newcomers arrived, these guides would help them get located for $100. The confusion began when more people came than land was available. In order to get the usual $100 for location, they would locate a newcomer on another man's property, and go on the next. Of course, this confusion caused much trouble; many times, killing.

I decided to buy my land. My sister Ada and I each bought twenty acres of the old Jim Farr Ranch where we now live. She lives over there in the next house. She only has two acres of land left. She traded eighteen acres of this city land for two-hundred acres out on Grape Creek where they are expecting an oil boom. They have some oil near her place.

You go over and let Ada show you her two-acre farm. She is an old maid also. You know, I am 80 years old and she is a few years younger. We don't live together—it takes the entire house for each of us. As you know, I'm blind, and when I place something I want it to stay there until I move it.

If I were to go over, she would start the chicken feud again. She is really sold on Barred Rock chickens and white turkeys. She will also show you a shoe box full of prize ribbons that she has won at different fairs. I always liked the game chickens—something that will stand up for its own rights. They caused so much confusion that I sold them.

I read and write for most of my pasttime. I use the paint and Braille system to read and correspond with my blind friends. I bought a typewriter and learned to write to my seeing friends.

I am very independent, even though some people say I'm handicapped. I do not get a pension. I didn't ask for it and don't want it. I am not like those people begging for relief.

It is about time for my exercise (reaching up to touch her Braille clock). You see I have the chicken wire all the way around the porch; I walk up and down for exercise.

My real name is Mattie or Martha. When I was a child about three years of age, I took a sudden dislike to my name because so many people called me Marthie instead of Martha. I liked the name of Babe and would not answer when called otherwise, so you must call me Babe instead of Miss Mattie.

Ruby Mosley
n.d.

Chapter 8 — Hardships

Mrs. Laura Hoover
Ozona, Crockett County

Laura Hoover helped to build, and lived in, the first house in Crockett County. She said, "In the so-called good old days, we watched the construction of our one-room mud house with one eye and looked for Indians with the other." She was called "Mother Hoover" by her friends, and that is the name she is listed under in the Federal Writers' Project.

We built our house under a big bluff, because we wanted the protection from the weather and also the Indians. Across this bluff just seven miles was a water well known as Howard's Well, but we could not cross that way and were forced to go entirely around, a distance of some twenty-five miles, to obtain our drinking water.

No mansion was ever constructed with greater fondness of pride or its occupancy enjoyed more fully, than was that first shelter from the black winds and blinding dust storms of the wild and woolly west. We made our foundation of cedar pickets and covered that with a mixture of mud and grass. The one big room had one window and one door.

Many times I have known periods of seven to ten months to elapse without my seeing a women of any kind, but I did not have to look around to find something to while away the time—no lonely hours for me. My duties with the household, the babies, and helping my husband with the round-ups and branding occupied my every moment much more fully than the bridge hours of today.

We hauled our supplies from Fort Stockton, and occasionally when they were exhausted there we would have to go on to Fort Davis.

We were 80 miles from a doctor and knew better than to get sick. I made tea from greasewood plant, and it served for practically all ailments. Risings of any sign of blood poisoning were treated with patalla poultices.

On one occasion when my husband was away, which he was very often, I was at work in the back of the house, when I looked up and saw a big rattler stretched across my door.

He was sunning himself contentedly and made no attempt to get away as I moved toward my rifle. I killed him and watched for his mate to show up for several days, but I never saw another snake that large.

I have been a widow now for several years but still try to have the home fires burning when the children or my many good friends visit my home.

Elizabeth Doyle
November 16, 1937

Mrs. J. D. Rylee
Granbury, Hood County

There was not only danger from Indians, but from wild Longhorn cattle and hogs which ran wild, too. I've seen wild hogs with tushes (tusks) four or five inches long, and they would certainly hurt you bad if they got the chance, and they would fight you. I have seen them fight dogs and just slash the dogs down with their tushes. But the dogs learned how to fight the hogs and jump out of reach of their tushes. It was dangerous for persons to go around much on foot. We all went armed with pistols, guns, and Bowie knives and rode good horses.

William V. Ervin
January 7, 1937

CHAPTER 9
Ranch Life

Miss Gula B. Foote
Ben Ficklin
and San Angelo, Tom Green County

Nellie B. Cox, an interviewer for the WPA, wrote the following account based on a diary kept by Miss Foote.

A pioneer girl of the West carried a revolver, rode bad horses, roped cattle, and herded sheep. These activities were not carried on in a spirit of bravado or daring but as part of the everyday work. Miss Gula B. Foote, who came to Ben Ficklin [Benficklin] in 1876, has done all of these things and has kept a diary of the things she thought of as ordinary happenings in a busy life.

Miss Foote's father, C.D. Foote, a civil engineer, came to the western part of Texas in 1875. The next year he sent to Michigan for his family, which consisted of his wife, who was a

Courtesy West Texas Collection, Angelo State University, San Angelo, Texas
Miss Gula B. Foote.

A Legacy of Words — Texas Women's Stories 1850-1920

teacher of piano in a large school; a daughter Gula, aged nine; and a small son, Harry.

Miss Foote tells in her diary:

"We had an uneventful train trip to Round Rock, Texas. There we were met by my father. We then traveled in a fearful (to mother and me) manner, that is, a brown-topped hack drawn by horses. We were afraid of everything—principally the horses—but we imagined worse things—Indians, rattlesnakes, and skunks. My father did all the cooking on the trip as my mother was never good in the culinary arts, even in the best-equipped kitchen. However, through it all I was thrilled to be going to our new home."

The diary relates that at an early age she overcame her fear of horses. She delighted to meet the stage at Ben Ficklin, for the driver, W. J. Ellis, after discharging the passengers, would permit Gula to drive the four horses hitched to the big stagecoach down to the corrals.

Miss Foote tells of riding broncos at fairs in competition with men riders and of winning. She always rode sideways, never astride. "White Bess," an Arabian mare owned by Mr. Foote, would permit no one except Gula to ride her.

After her father became disabled, Miss Foote took over the entire management of their ranch, which they named, "Kiowa Ranch." Here she bred, raised, and broke to saddle and harness the fine horses which were the best in show ring or in actual use. She gave them such names as "Lady Bird," "Chaquita," "Chico." Miss Foote had nothing but ridicule for "scrub stock."

On the ranch Miss Foote did all kinds of work, even milking the cows, which is always a distasteful job to any ranchman or ranchwoman. She tells that one Sunday a somewhat shiftless widower in the neighborhood stayed around the ranch all day. When milking time came and she started out with the milk buckets, the man sidled up to her and said soulfully, "Miss Gula, don't you ever feel the need of a man about the place?" "Yes," replied Miss Foote, "but when I do, I hire one."

The many mementos tell of her part in the social life of the "gay '90s" and earlier. Dance cards filled with the names of popular gentlemen, engraved cards, pressed flowers, photographs, and newspaper clippings attest to the fact that Miss

Chapter 9 — Ranch Life

Courtesy West Texas Collection, Angelo State University, San Angelo, Texas

Woman in front of tenant house on ranch,
possibly the Kiowa Ranch.

Foote was a much sought-after young lady in the society circles of Ben Ficklin and later of San Angelo.

After leasing out the ranch, Miss Foote sold her horses and moved to her home in San Angelo. She owned and learned to drive a car, but always insisted that she would much prefer driving her favorite team of ranch horses.

Mrs. Emma Kelly Davenport
Sabinal and Uvalde, Uvalde County

Mrs. Davenport tells about living on her father's ranch when she was a child, her courtship and marriage to a rancher, and their life together. She tells a poignant story about a child of hers dying from a rattlesnake bite.

Interviewer Mrs. Florence Fenley Angermiller added this comment to Mrs. Davenport's story: "As a young woman, she [Mrs. Davenport] had the uncommon trait of keeping diaries, keepsakes, and historical mementos. Belt buckles worn by her

A Legacy of Words — Texas Women's Stories 1850-1920

father and her husband's father as soldiers in the Confederacy, powder horns, and valuable documents contribute to the interesting lore of early days."

My mother, Nancy Williams, was born in Perry County, Illinois, the daughter of Milton Williams. Her grandfather, Robert Williams, fought under General George Washington in the Revolutionary War. When she was very young, her parents brought her to live in Arkansas, and there is where she later married my father, Chris Kelly, on December 24, 1847, near the town of Searcy in White County. In 1851, they moved to Kaufman County, Texas, and in 1853 they came to the Sabinal Canyon, where I was born nearly eleven years later, August 27, 1864.

You see, she was only about nineteen years old when she came out here, and though it was about a year before the Indians began giving them serious trouble, it became necessary after that, oft' times, for my mother to go to the field with my father and hold her baby and his gun while he worked.

My parents began ranching as soon as they got to the Sabinal Canyon. They had brought their horses and cattle and wagons with them, and other members of his family had come along, also. In fact, there was a train of them. One wagon was provided for my mother, and I think it was a little finer than the other wagons. She had her own bedding and personal things in that wagon.

My daddy had a mischievous brother along in the wagon train, and he tormented everything and everybody. His name was Jack Kelly. One day, he was riding in my mother's wagon and kept teasing her. She got tired of it after awhile and took off her shoe and threw it at him. She hit him right on the nose, and it sure drew the blood. My daddy would have whipped him right there, but the whole wagon train took up for him and wouldn't have stood for it, because they knew his mischief was all in fun.

The trip was made in ordinary time, but the roads those days were simply awful. Scarcely more than a trail over the rough mountains or across long-stretches of muddy prairie kept them from making more than eight or ten miles a day, lots of times. A heap of times, they had to lie over for the

Chapter 9 — Ranch Life

swollen creeks and rivers to go down, so they could cross.

My daddy was always in the saddle and was always with the other settlers on the cow hunts. In 1870, he decided to take a herd of cattle to California, so he and Gid Thompson went together and threw their herds together. Gid's two boys, Hy and Bob, went along. The reason for selecting California was because of there being so much money out there after that gold rush. Cattle here was fat, for they had open range and plenty of water. They knew it would take a long time to make that trip, so they prepared for it. They bought up different small herds around in the country and got together about 3,000 head.

John Davenport (whom I was later to marry) and others of the neighborhood stayed up at the ranch headquarters the night before the herd left on the trail. They went with the outfit for one day's travel. The last night we stayed at home, which was this same night the boys were all camped around to start before day the next morning. The camp was awakened by my father singing that old song:

"Wake up, wake up, you drowsy sleepers
Wake up, wake up, it's almost day!
How can you lie and sleep and slumber
When your true love is going away!'

I guess that was pretty hard on my mother, for she realized that he would be gone a year or two, if he came back alive at all. No one knew whether they would ever get through or not, and it was hard to give them up.

It took them two days to go from headquarters, here on the Sabinal, to Uvalde, and we camped one night with them on the way to Uvalde. I remember that one of the cowboys caught me up and stood me up on the sugar barrel next morning. It was a barrel of brown sugar they were taking along with their provisions.

My mother finally sold her home in Uvalde and moved back up to our ranch before my father ever returned from California. I was going to school up there, then. I have heard them talk about my father coming home by boat, so I suppose he took a train from California to St. Louis, and then went by boat down the Mississippi to New Orleans and then around by Galveston, for I do know that he landed at Galveston and came on up to Houston. It took him a long time to make that trip, and we hadn't had a letter from him in no telling when.

The day he came in, my mother had gone down below to stay all night with my oldest sister. She rode horseback down there and left me at a neighbor's house. I saw two men come up the road horseback, but I never knew it was my daddy till he went on home, and my brother came down in a run in a little while and told me that he was there. We had looked for him so long, I ran like a race horse to get to where he was.

I had forgotten about an old mean, fighting cow we had. We always had to keep out of her way, for she would run at you or fight anything. Well, I ran right into her face before I saw her. She tossed her head and I tossed over the fence. Gracious, I sure did run then. When I got to where I could see my daddy, he was standing in the door and when he saw me, he reached up and caught the top of the door facing and began dancing. I tell you, we were all so happy we couldn't behave. He got on his horse then and rode on down to my sister's where my mother was. They said it was a great meeting with mother crying and clinging to him. She just couldn't stop crying.

He brought back a mint of money from that trip and told many an interesting experience they had on their way out there. He said that old man Ben Biggs and his boys, Jim and Billy, were several hundred miles ahead of them with about six-hundred head of cattle. They had about the same experiences crossing the desert and strips of country without water as the Biggs' outfit had had. I heard him say that when they got to California and they needed to go into town—I think it was San Diego—and they were all so ragged and torn up and threadbare that none of them would have dared try to go into town looking like that. Not a one of them had a decent pair of pants left to go into town after provisions and clothes for the other fellows. But John Taylor met the emergency. He took the wagon sheet and cut out a pair of pants with a butcher knife. I suppose his leggings hid the stitches. I think they had a needle or two and some twine or coarse thread along. The boys thought it was a good idea. They were all so shaggy, with long hair and beard and so dirty they were longing to get into

Chapter 9 — Ranch Life

town for a clean-up. Well, John Taylor saved the day and went into town with his handmade duck pants, and he bought clothes for the other boys and brought them out so they could all go in to town.

After his return from California, my father began making preparations for another trip up the trail, this time to Kansas with a herd. Our lives were pretty easy from that time on for he made the trip and made lots of money. Then when he began making plans for a third trip, my mother set her foot down on it. She told him she was tired of staying alone and raising babies and calves while he was always gone. He didn't make the trip either.

As my father was strictly a stockman, he lived on a ranch till his death. In a few years after his cattle drives, he began experimenting with sheep and was very successful in handling them. I was partly fed on sheep meat, and as my winter clothing came from the sheep's back, I like sheep to this day.

I remember that sheep-shearing time was surely a busy time for us. Sometimes there would be fifteen or twenty shearers come at one time, and if the weather was good, they could soon do the work. They were generally Mexicans, and there nearly always was a musician with them. They are great people to sing and play a guitar, and we always loved to hear them. Once, there was a shearer with the crew who could imitate any kind of animal or bird he had ever heard. All of us children tried to do the same thing, and we certainly made a racket, if nothing else.

One day one of the shearers spoke to me in Spanish and said he was going to cut off one of my curls. I didn't understand him, and made a dash for the house, scared to death, and told my mother that he said he was going to cut my head off. After they found out why I ran, they laughed at the joke on me, and tried every way to make friends with me, but I stayed off at a distance and watched. Even their gifts of *peloncillos* (*pe-lon-cios*) [brown sugar candy] sent to me by my brothers didn't win my confidence any more.

I went to school mostly up where Utopia is now. As I grew up, I took part more and more in the programs we usually had on Friday afternoons, and we nearly always had visitors. Boys who liked certain school girls were pretty sure to be there. Two of my girl friends and myself got to where we expected certain boys to be there for the program. John Davenport always came after me on Friday evenings, and he would get me and his girl cousin in the buggy and go to the store. He would buy a pound of candy for us, and it would be wrapped up in paper, as we had never seen candy put up in boxes then. We would drive on to his cousin's house and let her out, then we would go back to my home. I lived a mile north of the school, and she lived a mile south of it, and though he always drove pretty, fine-trotting horses, I noticed he didn't hurry them after we let his cousin out of the buggy and started back to my home.

Our parents were always strict about letting us go anywhere, and we weren't allowed to go to parties on school days, only on Friday or Saturday nights. I was thinking lots of John Davenport about then, even though I was only 14 years old. I thought he was the handsomest thing I ever had seen, and I felt sure that he wanted to marry me, but he hadn't asked me yet. There was another girl over about D'Hanis that I knew he had been interested in, and I would hear different reports about it at times, but he seemed so much in love with me when we were together, I would always forget that there might be someone else.

The school days wore on toward an end that year, and I must confess that I made my worst grades. I had always made such good grades, but the last year I nearly failed. My mind was on John Davenport too much. However, I was very enthusiastic toward the close of the term and tried to catch up on my grades and practiced speeches and parts for the programs to be given at the close of school.

One afternoon, I was sitting under the arbor out at the side of the schoolhouse, and I don't suppose any one knew I was there. I happened to be looking right down the trail when I saw Andrew _____ meet his stepfather and kill him. It was an old score settled, for Andrew said his mother had been terribly mistreated, and he had told his stepfather that if he ever attempted to speak to him, he would kill him. Andrew's mother died, and his stepfather married again and was living with his second wife when Andrew killed him. I don't know what they said to each other, but Andrew shot him down, and there was a terrible confusion around there then, and somebody gave Andrew a horse to leave on. He pulled out right over to Uvalde and gave himself up. He didn't stay in jail very long, and when he was tried, he came clear.

Well, at the close of the last year of my schooling, we had a May Party. On a vote, I was elected queen, and all the attendants were chosen. I remember that I was all dressed up in a white organdy with fluted ruffles. They took our old piano box and decorated it up with flowers for a throne. I had flowers on me, too, and my attendants were all decorated with flowers. When all the girls came in and made their speeches to me and handed me their septres and wands, I jumped up and said,

"AMEN!

And heaven support us too!

'Tis much we mighty people have to do—"

There was more to it and I went right through the whole speech, but my eye was roving over the crowd to see if a certain cowboy had arrived. Being fixed up my prettiest, it was natural that I wanted him to see that ceremony where I was crowned queen.

A little later that evening, I got a letter from him saying that on that day he would be taking a bunch of cattle to San Antonio and didn't think he could possibly get there. I was the worst disappointed girl in the world. But after all, he did get there before it was all over, and we went to a dance from there. We didn't stay late, because my father objected to dances at a public place.

They never let us go to every dance that come along, either. I remember I had a hard time getting to go to all the dances I wanted to. I have gone with my brothers horseback, far and near, and have even ridden behind them on their horse just to get to go. Of course, that would only be for a short distance, but no matter how close a dance was, we most always rode horseback to it. My parents gave a dance occasionally, and they were always largely attended. It was customary to dance nearly all night, and they would serve coffee and cake or cookies through the night to the guests. And how they could dance! They were always so graceful on the floor, and I do know that John Davenport was the most graceful dancer I ever saw. I just thought I was IT if I could dance with him.

He was rather timid in his younger days, and while he was with me, he didn't ask me to marry him. He waited till he left and was on a cow hunt down the country, then wrote me a letter. He said he had meant to ask me but his heart failed him, and he had been told that my parents objected to my marrying anyway. I wrote him back that I intended to marry whom I wanted and would not try to please my parents about it if a question arose. We considered ourselves engaged then, and I was only 14, as I told you. He came to see me as often as he could, but he nearly always came in a buggy so he could take me places.

John Davenport and I married in 1878, and the first two or three years of our married life, we lived on a cow ranch. We had stock of our own and were on my father's place on the Sabinal River. I reckon I have lived on at least seven or eight different places on the Sabinal River. We run the J W D brand, which was John's brand when we married. The J was on the shoulder, the W on the side, and the D on the hip. My brand was EMA on the side, for you see I had stock of my own on my father's ranch, too.

John continued on the cow hunts. The country was not entirely fenced up yet, and they used to go on roundups and take pack-horses along. They would take a sack of biscuits, some bacon and coffee, sometimes a frying pan and coffee pot. If it was a lasting job, they probably would take two pack-horses to the outfit and maybe a wagon. They would round up from the head of the Sabinal and go down the country a good ways and meet other outfits that were on the east and west. I have seen many a roundup thrown together, and I have seen the ranchmen marking and branding at the round-ups and driving their stock home. Everybody was after the mavericks. The first man to get his rope on him got him. They have penned in our corrals many a time, but they hardly ever come to the house for their meals because they had their own camp outfit with them. You would see all those cowboys and men with their guns on them working right along in the hot dusty pens. Most ranchmen kept their girls and wives away from the pens when an outfit was working there, and most of them hardly ever went to the pens except for some home work where they were needed awhile.

Chapter 9 — Ranch Life

If the cow hunts went on longer then was expected, John would generally ride in again in two or three days and get some more biscuits. He kept a sack tied on his saddle. They would ride all day, and when they went to eat, they would always have fresh beef and biscuits.

We pre-empted a place of our own and went to running sheep with our cattle. I was used to sheep and loved to handle them. We nearly raised six of our children on that place before they were old enough to go to school. The children were always tickled to death when their daddy would ride in after he had been gone awhile. I always felt like I was one of the children myself, I was so young when I married. At least, he petted me as much as he did one of the children, and we were sweethearts all our married life.

While the children were small, we would have to move closer to school at times or maybe to town, then move back to the ranch. But we kept a teacher at home when they were right little.

We had a governess there the time we lost our little boy. We had gone out on the river that day, and the children were all playing around. Little Georgie went to climb up on a log while they were running around, and there was a rattlesnake lying under it. It bit him on the ankle, and we grabbed him up right then and bound his leg and started for the doctor. One of the boys ran to the house and got a chicken, and we split it open and laid it on the bite. John drove the horses in a run, and I sat in the back and held him and I also held that chicken on his little ankle. We got to the doctor and he did everything that could be done or that he knew to do. We worked with him all night, but we lost him just at sunrise the next morning.

I talked to that doctor later, and he told me he had never lost but one other child from a snake bite since that time. My next baby was a girl, and I named her Georgia as a namesake of the little one we lost.

We used to do lots of our visiting after supper. Many a time, we have gone to see my mother or John's mother after supper or maybe to some neighbor's. We always went in a buggy or a hack. I think back now on how I used to go with John down to his mother's place east of Sabinal, and the next morning we would be hurrying to get off, and I never helped with the breakfast dishes or any of the work. She insisted that she would clean up after we got off, but I wouldn't do that now if it was to do over.

John loved to sing, and he loved music in every way. His mother liked music the same way, and she could play the violin pretty good. She always loved to see her children and grandchildren come and always had something good for them to eat. She lived on the highway between San Antonio and Sabinal, about two miles east of the present town of Sabinal.

For years she kept a store there, and the freighters and travelers always stopped with her. There is where I saw so many ox trains and mule trains pass by. Freighters hauled cotton to Mexico in season, and I have seen bales piled up on the wagons as long as they could get one on. Sometimes the Mexicans would come by from Mexico with *peloncillos* to sell. And I have seen them peddling redbirds, just ordinary redbirds that are wild. You could put them in a cage and feed them cracked corn and water, and they would just whistle and whistle for you. Those peddlers oft' times had fancy needlework and beautiful drawn work that must have taken them weeks to make. It was always rather cheap, too. The country was getting more thickly settled then, and the menace of Indians was over.

We stayed in the sheep business up to the last few years of John's life. We put in a two-hundred acre farm at the foot of the hills and continued on with our cattle and sheep. Later, we leased out our farm and ranch and moved to Sabinal to this home I live in now and where John died in 1926. All of our ten children were there: Jim, Raymond, McCormick, Connie (who died a short while after), Rollie, Lila, Georgia, Ira, Davie, and Newell. Since he passed away, I have been blessed with having the children all around me. I miss the old life, and I love to see all the old-timers in this country whenever we can. I have long wanted a record made of these things I have told you, and that is why I have preserved dates and other information which I have showed you.

Mrs. Florence Angermiller
March 14, 1938

Chapter 9 — Ranch Life

Mrs. Lizzie Powers
Marlin, Falls County,
and Mart, McLennan County

After I married [in 1883], I lived on the ranch in Falls County, which was ten miles north of Marlin. I lived there about twenty years. By this time, the railroad had reached Marlin, and we sent our cattle there to be shipped by train to the northern markets. The Powers brothers who remained on the ranch worked together and marketed their herds together. The range was owned by individuals, but there were wild cattle that were rounded up with the ranch herds. Sometimes a small bunch of ranch cattle were herded out in the open range on moonlit nights to draw the wild cattle, scattered in the timber, into these herds. The wild cattle belonged to the one who first put a brand on them.

A man did not need much money to buy a herd in those days, for cattle were cheap. A big beef steer would sell for around ten dollars. Only enough money was needed to bear the expenses of rounding up the cattle and taking them to market. I have heard how, when they were driven up the trail, the inspector was first notified. After he came and inspected them, he would tally them, and the road brand would be placed on each cow. The inspector gave the trail boss a pass on his herd to show they had been inspected. The inspector put the tally on record in the county clerk's office. Other cattlemen could look at this record, and if they found any cattle with their mark or brand, the owner of the herd would pay him for what he had rounded up and that belonged to the other fellow, if he was an honest man.

About 1901, we moved to Edwards County and lived fifteen miles from Rocksprings, the nearest post office. Our nearest market was Kerrville, a distance of ninety miles over very rough, rocky roads and mountains. Kerrville is about seventy-five miles northwest of San Antonio, on the Guadalupe River. To this town, we had to send our produce by wagon train, to which from six to eight head of horses were driven. In making the trip, the Guadalupe River was crossed eleven times, due to the winding of the road. The country was wild and beautiful.

We had a stock ranch and raised sheep, goats, cattle and horses; some grain, mostly enough to feed the stock. It was a common thing to meet people who had never seen cotton grow, or had seen a train.

As for Negroes, one time one came to Rocksprings, and it was like a circus with the people coming to see him.

Rattlesnakes were numerous. There were many, under every rock, but few fatalities, for people knew their hiding places and kept away.

I have lived on the ranch for months without seeing another woman.

Miss Effie Cowan
n.d.

Mrs. Arthur B. Duncan
Clarendon, Donley County, and Floydada, Floyd County

The conflict between cattlemen and "nesters" was real to Mrs. Duncan, who was harassed by a cowboy until she pointed a Winchester rifle at him. Her husband was later elected the first county judge of Floyd County.

"Recollections of A Pioneer Mother"
(By Mrs. Arthur B. Duncan, first settler of Floyd County)

> Little dugout home so lowly
> Knew you not that in your keeping
> Dwelt the builders of a nation
> The beginning of a people?
> As they heard the wild birds calling
> Love notes at the mating season
> Love, between a man and maiden,
> Built the first homes in the West.
> Years have passed, and from their labor
> Now a West of strength and beauty
> Rises forth in all its splendor

Chapter 9 — Ranch Life

> Like a bright Celestial City,
> But when evening's sun is sinking
> And the world is wrapped in shadow
> Seems I hear the West Wind sighing
> For those little dugout homes.

With my husband and my seven-month-old son, I left Montague County on the first day of March in the year 1884, to go to that part of the plains now known as Floyd County, to file on a homestead. With us went an orphan boy whose name was Bob Prince. We were on the road three months, reaching our destination on June first of that year.

Our road was little more than a trail for the greater part of this long journey. There had been little commerce or transportation into this new country. Sometimes, when we would get too tired to sit longer in the wagon, we would get out and walk beside the trails, with Bob driving the wagon.

I remember one experience during this trip, which has remained vividly in my mind throughout the years that followed as typical of the many emergencies we were to meet in the months ahead. In Wichita County, still many miles from our destination and from any sign of human habitation, we were going down the old McKenzie trail. My husband and I were walking beside the wagon, as the horses were having hard going. Continued travel over the trail had worn the ruts so deep that we had traveled for hours without an opportunity to turn out. We told Bob to watch for a chance to turn out, but to be careful, but when he pulled out of the trail, the [wagon] tongue snapped in two.

Arthur said, "What are we going to do?" I said: "We have a saw and a hammer and some nails and some bed slats. We will fix it." And we did, so well, in fact, that we used it for several years before that tongue was ever replaced with another.

I don't think I shall ever remember anything more beautiful than my first sight of the plains. It was at the time of the year when nature is at her best in this country. The trees in the canyon were green. The whole region looked untouched by the hand of man. As we drove along, we saw great white mounds of buffalo bones, piled there by the men who had killed the buffalo for the hides, leaving the bones to bleach. Later, these were gathered up and shipped to eastern factories to be used in making fertilizer.

We saw very few live buffalo. There were occasional small herds of antelope, beautiful timid creatures that ran on sight of our invading wagon. Coyotes were plentiful and often came quite close to our wagon or our camp. We had to watch out for rattlesnakes, too. Sometimes we would find them directly in our trail, barring further passage until they had been disposed of, or sunning on the rocks in the canyon.

Our first stop after coming up on the caprock was the home of Hank Smith, still known as the "Rock House." They had been here fifteen years when we came. We made camp, and I went up to the house to get some milk and thus met Mrs. Hank Smith for the first time. She very kind to us and extended to us the same hospitality for which she has always been known. They lived in what is known as Crosby County, and she was one of the first to live in that county.

We stayed there by the rock house for nearly three months before my husband found a site on which he wanted to establish our homestead. The State was giving this land to settlers who would live on it for three years. We drove our wagon down to the place he had chosen, made camp, and then he set out for Clarendon to file on the land, leaving me there to hold the site while he was gone. I felt very much alone away off down there in the canyon, in a strange country, without any protection except my own and what meager assurance the fourteen-year-old Bob could offer.

As night came on, a black cloud began to come up in the west, and Bob came to the wagon to say that he had found a sheepherder's dugout a short distance away where he thought we had better go, as it was going to "rain the bottom out" by the time night fell. I hated to go, but as the cloud grew nearer and blacker I decided that it would be better. I was afraid the sheepherder would come in and find us trespassing on his property. The storm was terrible, and we were glad we had sought better shelter than our wagon.

As it grew dark inside the dugout, Bob cut down some dried pieces of meat which were hung from the ceiling and made a fire of them. This gave us both light and heat, for

Chapter 9 — Ranch Life

which we were extremely grateful. When it was quiet again outside, we climbed out of the dugout and went back to the wagon.

The next day Bob went back to the dugout, and under the sheepherder's bed, which was hung from the top of the dugout, he found a big rattlesnake. I was certainly glad we had decided not to sleep in that dugout.

The next five days passed quickly enough, but I shall never forget how glad I was to see my husband come riding in at the end of the fifth day. He had lost his hat in a dust storm. He was tired and dusty and hungry, but he had the necessary papers for our homestead, and we were ready to make plans for our new home.

Early the next morning, however, we had a caller. A cowboy came up to the wagon and told us that they wanted to see him, my husband, down at the corral, which he indicated was only a short distance down the canyon from our camp. They were men of the T M Bar ranch and were English landowners and cattlemen. The land on which we had filed happened to be on some of their range. Of course, stockmen in that day had it in for the "nesters," as they called them, and I was afraid for Arthur to go down there where they were.

I said "Arthur, are you going down there with nothing to defend yourself?" and he replied, "I am not afraid of them" and went ahead. When he got down to the corral, the boss of the outfit asked him just how he proposed to make a living. He told them it was "none of their danged business." When they found that they could not discourage him or intimidate him, they announced that they would "scare his woman" and would finally drive us off in that way.

We moved into the sheepherder's dugout where I had taken refuge from the storm on that first night. The sheepherder who had built the place had belonged to the T M Bar ranch, and they warned us that we were not to disturb either the dugout or any of the equipment or supplies we might find in it. But we went ahead, moving his things out into a corner of a shelter we had built for our few chickens, thus further antagonizing our closest neighbors.

One morning I heard my shepherd dog making a furious racket outside. I went to the door and opened it just in time to let the dog run in and escape the lasso with which a cowboy was trying to rope him. They knew my husband was gone all day caring for his flock of sheep, and they were trying to frighten me by abusing my dog. The cowboy was coming so fast that he was barely able to stop his horse in time to keep him from coming right into my dugout.

He rode away without a word from either of us, but that night when my husband came home, I told him all about it, and he said he would see that I was ready for such a visit next time. He loaded up his big Winchester for me and placed it right by the door with instructions to use it if I needed to.

The next day I heard the dog barking again, and when I looked out I saw the cowboy was luring him away from the house by making him chase his horse. When he thought he was far enough away from the house, he whirled his horse and began to chase the dog, his rope turning above his head. The dog beat him to the dugout, however, and when the cowboy came up to the door he dismounted. I was ready for him. I picked up my gun and pointed it at him. Then I said, "Young man, do you think you are any part of a gentlemen? If you do, you will get yourself across to the other side of this canyon and stay there, or I'll fill you full of lead." That cowboy never bothered me again, although they annoyed us whenever possible.

The weeks in our dugout home grew quickly into years. We had little contact with the outside world. I never saw a woman for months at a time. We got our mail at Uncle Hank Smith's in those days. The Rock House was the center for any commerce with the outside world. He was the Indian Agent for that territory and we often saw tall, gaunt Indians walking down through the hills of the canyon, on their way to see Uncle Hank and get passes to other reservations. We did see a few tepees on some of our excursions through the country. They were strongly made of buffalo hides and looked as though they might last forever, but they finally disappeared; some of them, no doubt, being torn down by prospectors passing through the country.

We had lived there about three years when a preacher came into our country. He was a little preacher, the name of Duncan, and he was a Methodist Circuit Rider. Word was

Chapter 9 — Ranch Life

sent out through all the region round about that we were going to have a camp meeting. People were few and far between, and about thirty people in all attended that meeting. They came from Crosby, Dickens, Motley, and Floyd Counties. Some of the Quakers from the old settlement of Estacado came, also, to help us with the meeting.

We all got together and built a beautiful little tree arbor down in the canyon by the river. It was a wonderful thing to all of us to be able to mix and mingle with other people again. I especially enjoyed two of the Quaker girls who were about my own age; I was a very young woman still, and I had many long, lonely days of solitude behind me in the three years since I had come to my new home. We would go off down the river between services and talk and pick the wild plums and currants and algerita berries from which we would make jelly for the winter months.

There was one incident, which happened during this meeting, which I am sure none of those present will ever manage to entirely forget. I had been glad to extend the hospitality of our humble home to all of the visiting people we could accommodate, and my supplies, which had not allowed for such an emergency, were running low. It was nearly time for one of the trips to Colorado City which the men made twice a year, to take down the crop of wool and bring back six-months' provision of flour, sugar, molasses, and coffee, with whatever things were considered indispensable to this primitive way of living.

I had several guests that morning for breakfast and I had put forth my best efforts and most of my remaining supplies to make it as nice as I could for them. But just as I had put it all on the table and turned to call my company in, I noticed that dirt was falling from the ceiling above. As I looked, the dirt fell faster, and then in a cascade that completely covered my table. My husband was standing in the door of the dugout and saw what was happening, and as we looked, we saw the hind leg of a big steer come through the top of our dugout. He had wandered down from the caprock above and had fallen through our roof.

Well, of course, the breakfast was ruined, but there was nothing to do but face the situation as we had faced countless others. Arthur said, "Mother, what are we going to do?" I said, "Why, get a shovel and let's unload this dirt" and that was the only thing we could do, except rescue the steer and repair the roof.

My husband's brother, Wood Duncan, had settled some miles up the canyon from us. He was very kind to us and helped us over many hard places. I shall never forget him and his old sourdough bucket which always went with him on his sheep herding expeditions. He was a good cook and was always cook for the outfit when they all got together during shearing time or on other occasions which demanded the services of more than one man. When he killed a sheep, he always brought us a "ham of mutton".

About the only kind of pies we could have in those days were vinegar pie. He would buy the vinegar in huge barrels. One day he gave me a bottle of vinegar, and I put it on some beets which I had raised in a little garden I had managed to get started. When it came off it was a beautiful red. We had so little color in those days that I thought that jar of vinegar was the prettiest thing I ever saw. One day I had a guest for dinner and I determined to use the vinegar for a pie. He insists to this day that that was the best and the prettiest pie he has ever eaten.

We were always glad to have any company, and to offer food and lodging to any wayfarer who passed our way. One day an old Mexican woman, riding a burro, and her son came to our door, and by means of signs and grunts asked for food and a place to sleep. We could not understand any of their speech and they could not understand us, but we had them come in, gave them supper and a place to sleep, and the next morning sent them on their way, not regretting our hospitality in the least.

But more was to come. We began to notice the little crawling things known as cooties hopping out of our clothing and jumping about nearly every place we happened to look. Our guests had left us a generous supply in payment for our kindness. I didn't know what to do to get rid of them, but Wood told us to put all the bed clothing and everything movable out in the sun, and that the ants would eat them up. I did this, but I could not be content until I had washed everything that was washable and had aired them all thoroughly until we were finally rid of them.

We would sometimes see a man or a group of men, walking down a wild horse or mustang. These men were called horse hunters and they caught these wild plains horses by the simple expedient of walking them until they were too tired to go farther, or trapping them in some canyon from which they were not clever enough to escape.

I remember one mustang in particular, which two horse hunters had trapped, or thought they had at least, in a place close to our dugout. He was the handsomest horse I have ever seen, a great dapple-grey stallion. He was almost exhausted when night fell, but he climbed a bluff, a feat which appeared impossible, and escaped for awhile longer. I never learned whether they caught him or not, but these men were persistent, and I feel sure that they finally accomplished his capture.

Rattlesnakes, coyotes, and skunks were our ever-present neighbors, and we learned to keep out of their way whenever possible. Sometimes the coyotes would venture quite close to the house, and my small son would seat himself on a big white rock just outside the door, armed with a butcher knife, and announce that he "would take care of me."

Our house was usually security enough from all these dangers, but it was not always proof against the heavy rains. When it had rained just so much, the water would begin to seep through the top of the dugout, and I would have to cover the bed with a tarpaulin, and put coats over the babies to keep as dry as possible until it was over.

One evening after a heavy rain, my husband came in from his day with the sheep and found us so. He stopped in the door, and at the sorry sight we presented, all the discouragements of the months behind seemed to come to his mind and he said in a pathetic way, "See what you got into by marrying me." I gave him a grin and told him that if we never had anything worse than that to contend with, we would get through fine. And we did.

Our first little girl, the first girl baby born in Floyd County, was born in the beginning of our third year on our homestead. She was frail and fair and seemed entirely too delicate to ever survive in such rugged surroundings. Arthur was so proud of her. He called her "the lily of the canyon and the rose of all the plains." We had few of the things that are considered necessary to the rearing of children in these days, but they grew strong and sturdy on what we had to give them.

With this increase in our family, I needed another bed for the dugout. I had no material with which to make one, except some tow sacks. In those days the sacks were used for taking wool to the market, and were much stronger and more closely woven than those of today. I pulled some of the threads from the sacks to use for thread to sew them with, and when I had it all made, I went down to the river and cut me some of the tall grass to fill it with. When I had it all filled, I thought that that mattress, made of clean tow sacks and filled with new-mown hay, was the sweetest smelling bed I had ever seen.

This grass, by the way, grew in profusion in the lakes, and in the dry season the men would cut and bale it for hay for winter feed. When the grass was cut, you could sometimes see the "salt licks" where the buffalo had come down and licked the alkaline spots for salt.

The first three years we spent in the canyon, we had no cows. It was next to impossible to obtain milk for any purpose. So it was that when, at the end of that time, Zack Maxwell, my husband's brother-in-law, came our way, we were almost as overjoyed to see the three cows he was bringing with him, as we were to see him and to have word from home. Two of the cows were his, and the other one my mother was sending to me. All three had calves; I was so proud of mine that I hated for night to come and take them from my sight.

The next morning we were out bright and early, but my calf was nowhere to be seen. It had wandered off down the canyon and had fallen into a shallow well and drowned. This was a real tragedy to me. It took me a long time to get over the loss of my calf.

Zack Maxwell had come to settle in this country, and he located in Plainview, the first settler at that place, although it did not bear that name until later.

My twin brother, J. J. Day, then came to make his home in this region, and settled some seven or eight miles above us in what is now known as Starkey. My mother, a widow, and a survivor of other pioneer days, came to make her home with him. They lived there for many years and for a long time ran the post office; his wife, Mattie Day, taking care of all mail for the entire country round about.

One day, when Arthur had gone over to Estacado on business, he sent me word by a cowboy that he could not get back that night. Bob, who still made his home with us, was off with the sheep. I had never had to stay alone at night, and I felt that I just could not do it. So I went out, hitched the horses to the wagon, and got ready to go over to my brother's house. But my plans did not work out.

The men had taken the bed out of the wagon and had put in long poles for hauling hay. I started out, however, putting my babies back of me on the poles, but they were not heavy enough to hold the poles in place. The poles began to slip out and the babies with them, so I had to go back and spend the night alone.

This experience was hardly as bad as one which another pioneer woman of my later acquaintance recalled, however. One night when her husband failed to come home, she went out to look for her cows, and when night fell, found that she was lost. She was afraid to stay in one place, for fear some wandering cows might run over some of the children, so she walked all night, carrying the baby and with the other children holding on to her skirts.

When morning came, she found that she had stumbled, exhausted, up to about three-hundred yards of her home. In the dark she had been unable to see it. The woman was Mrs. Van Leonard whom many early settlers will remember and who resides in Floydada today.

As time went on, my growing family needed new clothes. I used to take the big flour and sugar sacks and make garments out of them. Sometimes I was able to dye them and make little girls' pretty dresses. For thread I used ravelings from "Sea Island" domestic. These sacks were of a strong, heavy quality and made substantial garments.

We had to be careful and watchful of our needles, of course, for the loss of one was a misfortune that could not be very quickly remedied. I do not remember my own record as to keeping a needle, but Mrs. D. D. Shipley, an early-comer to

Floyd County, once told me that she kept and used one needle for seven years.

I made every effort possible to make our dugout home attractive and livable. I nailed tow sacks to the walls and covered them with newspapers. These made a clean surface, on which the light was more easily captured from our one window, and they could by changed as often as need be. My dugout had two compartments, the kitchen and the bedroom or "parlor."

One day a family camped down near us, and the lady came up to see if she could borrow my coffee grinder. Of course, I was glad to loan it to her and asked her into my home. She had never seen such a dwelling before, and, since I had put in so many untiring efforts to make it as attractive as possible, I was naturally proud of it and expected her to make some nice comment. What she said was, "Oh, but isn't it snaky down here?" I was too stricken to answer for a moment, but I finally recovered enough to say that I supposed it looked that way to her, but that it was the best home I had.

I usually went with my husband to milk the cows. One day when we had finished the evening's milking and were coming back to the dugout, we saw a skunk on the path just ahead of us. We had never had an encounter with one at such close range. Arthur handed me the milk buckets, got him a long stick and said he would kill it. He followed it for a short distance down the canyon, giving it sharp little blows. Presently he hit it hard on the head. The next thing I knew he was calling me loudly, and I dropped the milk buckets and ran to him as quickly as I could to see what was wrong. He had thought the skunk was dead, had stooped to inspect his "kill" and had received a full dose of the "skunk medicine" right in the eyes. He was completely blinded for several hours.

Later on, in our home in Floydada he was to have an experience quite as bad. Our cellar door was a trap door, opening only from the outside. One afternoon the children had come in with the news that a skunk was in the cellar. He went down to see about it, with me at his heels. He sent me back for a hoe to kill it with. I handed him the hoe, and then in my excitement, shut the cellar door, leaving him alone to face his enemy in the dark. I soon realized from his remarks what I had done, and I let him out before any serious damage was done.

Delise McGuire
July 22, 1936

Mrs. Mary Leakey Miles
Leakey, Real County, and Uvalde, Uvalde County

This introduction was written by Mrs. Florence Angermiller, WPA interviewer, following an interview on October 25, 1937: "Mary Leakey Miles, daughter of John Leakey [pronounced Lake-y], pioneer settler of the Frio Canyon and founder of the town of Leakey, Texas, is 70 years old and lived the life of the pioneer women of that day. She was born in 1867 at Leakey and grew up in the saddle, helping her father with the stock and riding the sidesaddle on horses scarcely broke.

"Her father, a tall, blue-eyed, red-complexioned man, feared nothing and lived daily by his brawn. Old-timers remember his use of profane language and tell how he pointed an empty revolver at Indians and cursed them till they fled. He ruled his household with a firm and imperious hand. Ten children of his own learned to ride, rope, and shoot under his expert guidance, nor were they spared the hard-fisted rule of their father. In site of thieving Indians, the old man prospered, and his children had their individual brands for their stock.

"Mary Leakey was the second daughter of the family. She was a tall, blonde girl whose horseback riding was unexcelled and who remembers her horses with fondness that is a mark of those who depended on a horse, much of the time for safety as well as toil.

"She married Virgle Miles in [1888?] and is the mother of eleven children. Her husband used her brand, ML, for a number of years, as she already had stock running under her own brand.

"Mrs. Miles resides in Uvalde on North Getty Street. Her husband died about twelve years ago, and since then she has sold her ranch holdings and is spending her old age in town."

A Legacy of Words — Texas Women's Stories 1850-1920

The town of Leakey was named for my father. He rode the first wagon trail ever, up in that country, and he was one of the first settlers ever to go up there. Two Ball boys and a single fellow by the name of Stamford went there with him.

Our first house in Leakey was built by my father and his help. It was a two-room house made of cypress boards cut from native cypress trees. There was a large fireplace in one end of the house, and we cooked over the fire in this fireplace. We had a hook hanging from the chimney that we hung iron pots on, and we used a Dutch oven and other skillets. Many a good meal of fine venison steaks and hot biscuits, as well as beef, was cooked in that old fireplace.

I used to ride on the range, but I couldn't rope like my sister could. That was one thing I never learned to do so well. We had brothers to do that, but my sister was nearly as good. I never helped with the round-ups as much as I worked with the stock about the place. My father used to send cattle out north of there. I don't know where they went to but guess some buyer come in and taken them north.

I've had horses run away with me and throw me, too. I went on crutches a whole year from a horse throwing me and another one stepping on me. It broke some ligaments loose in my ankle someway. One horse run about a mile once and I couldn't stop him, but my brother headed him off and caught him.

Pat was my favorite horse. He was a red roan. I thought he was awful smart but of course he belonged to me. He saved me from the Indians one time. It happened between the Frio River and what we call the Spring Branch. I wasn't far from my sister when the Indians run at us. My sister heard the cracking of the horses' hoofs and hollered to me, "Better go home!" and we broke and run. She went one way and I went the other, because I was afraid they'd cut me off from the crossing. They were not an alarm given; they would have caught and carried us off rather than have us give an alarm. They were after horses. They run us about two miles, but we were riding good horses and we outrun 'em.

My brother had one horse that was awful mean, and every chance we had, we would swipe him and ride 'im to see what we could with 'im.

Chapter 9 — Ranch Life

My sister, Mattie, just older than me, could ride, rope, and shoot as good as anybody I ever saw. I've seen her on some pretty mean horses, riding her sidesaddle, but she could sure handle 'em. She did most of her roping when she was helping in the pens. She'd take after a yearling anywhere and run it down and catch it, too. She could talk Mexican as good as any Mexican. She could break horses and was successful in a way. She never got hurt, but I got hurt twice.

I was trying to lead a horse behind the horse I was riding and got jerked off my horse, and it crippled me in the ankle again, though not so bad as when the horse stepped on me.

The boys used to help the girls up on their horses when they rode the sidesaddles. You put your foot in his hand and gave a spring. It was easy to spring up. We rode to church horseback. We went in wagons, too, but we traveled more by horseback in the early days. I have carried my children with me horseback when I rode the sidesaddle. I never would ride a man's saddle till my boy was sent to France, and then I never could face to go through town that way.

My second brother, Tom Leakey, was the best rifle and pistol shot I ever saw. I have seen him whirl his pistol with his finger in the guard and shoot ever' time the gun came over. He never missed his mark. He could throw things up and hit them before they could come down. He was a fine rifle shot, too.

I can't say which of my three brothers was the best roper, but we had a man working for us by the name of Bill Wall that was the best roper on the range or in the pens I believe I ever saw. I have seen him rope many a wild cow.

I have had a few run-ins with bad cattle myself. There was a range bull one time that was pretty bad. We sure had to keep on the watch for him. I've seen some real bull fights in my day. They'd gore each other till their entrails fell out.

About the worst bull fight I ever saw was between a black-and-white spotted one, and the other was a red one. We heard 'em coming. They were bellerin' a long ways off, and when they run together, they meant business. They fought till one of 'em killed the other one. He ripped him open and his entrails fell out. They had awful keen horns and when they were mad, they'd gore nearly anything that crossed their path.

We had mostly rail fences around our place. (Most of the rail fences in this section are cedar poles.) We had one piece of rock fence. We had to work then. We carried water, washed clothes, made soap, milked lots of cows, and cooked for big outfits all the time. Anytime a person stopped and hadn't had anything to eat, it had to be got for him.

That was a wild and unsettled country in those days. The thick cedar breaks and dense timber was a fine hideout for men and wild animals, too. Oh, I've heard panthers scream across those canyons, my goodness! You'd think it was a woman screaming unless you knowed. My oldest boy killed one on the head of the Dry Frio that was the biggest one I ever saw. He had it thrown across his horse and its nose was touching the ground on one side and his tail on the other side.

Albert laughed and said it was the biggest panther he ever killed. I told him, "Of course, it is. It's your first!"

CHAPTER 10
Town Life

Mrs. Emma Kelly Davenport
Uvalde, Uvalde County

Emma's father moved his family from their ranch to the town of Uvalde when he left on a long cattle drive in 1870, because Indians were such a threat.

My father left us a new wagon and team of horses and money enough to live on two years. He left us in a rented house, and after he was gone about two months, my mother built a new house in the west part of town, near where the Main Street School is now. We had taken everything we had from the ranch except a few milk cows and some hogs.

I was soon old enough to go to school, and my first school days were at Uvalde. My teacher was old Judge McCormick. He was gray-headed and a middle-aged man then, and all his days didn't change his appearance much. He was tolerably strict in school, but he was a great sport when it come to attending horse races or other sports. He was a great drinker, too. I remember he was always ready for ball games, and he said that John Davenport could throw a ball farther than any man he ever saw.

He told me that he never went to school over six months in the year in his life, and that a boy could get a good education if he would go six months and really try to learn. He said his school came in three-months' sessions at a time. He taught many a person in this country, and he trained lots of men to different trades. He was a good surveyor, and he taught that trade to John Davenport. They surveyed out many a section in this country, and my understanding is that they helped survey out the town of Uvalde. He had a fine compass and Jacob's staff and chain, and before the old Judge died, he presented that very same compass to my husband, and now it is owned by my son, Rollie Davenport. It is a fine instrument and as good as ever.

After my father was gone awhile, my sister, Sarah, married George Dillard, and George's sister married at the same time, so they had a big double wedding and "infair." That was down in the Patterson settlement on the Sabinal. I think everybody in the country came and helped celebrate.

It was at this very place, later on, that George Dillard dubbed me a tomboy, because I could run like a race horse. I could outrun any of the school boys in the whole country, unless it was Charley Harper, and I could run right with him. George Dillard decided to put a pair of pants on me, and I had always been taught it was a disgrace for a girl to put on men's clothing, so naturally I felt that I would be disgraced for life it such a thing were done. Well, he set out after me one day to catch me, but he would have had to be horseback to have done it. I took to the open pasture and I remember going over hills and down them, as I circled around to get back to the house. He found out he couldn't catch me. Not having any sisters near my age, I had played with the boys in their games till I was a good runner.

We stayed down at the Patterson settlement a few months after my sister married. We felt safer down there than we did at Uvalde. We were scared to death the whole time we lived in Uvalde. That certainly was a wild place, if there ever was one. Rangers and soldiers would come in there and get on wild sprees. They would get into fights and shoot up the town. It surely wasn't safe to go up town after dark. I've gone under the bed many a time when I was little and all that shooting was going on.

Once, there was a terrible commotion and shooting uptown, and the next morning we found out the cause of it. Two gamblers by the name of Asberry and Young were killed. They were men who had not been living there long and had no families. They were hard drinkers and gamblers and got into a fight with each other. Men would fall out with their very best friends in a gambling game. One of the men drew his gun and killed the other, and they took both of them to jail, the dead one and the wounded one. But someone went to jail and killed the other one.

It wasn't an uncommon thing for a cowboy fight or soldier-and-ranger fight to occur uptown. There were saloons and places for them to have trouble, and it often happened. There were so many outlaws and bad men in through here then, that men in this section went armed for years; the old and young—even boys 12 and 13 years old had pistols buckled on them. Many a time when a killing occurred, the killer ran away, and more often than not, made a clean get-away.

My mother's life was a busy one after we moved to Uvalde. She had a bunch of children to care for, and the cooking, mending, sewing, soapmaking, washing, ironing, and milking cows went right on. She started a garden right at once after we moved there, and she bought the first cook stove I ever saw. It didn't lack much of being the first one in the town, either. That stove had the regular four eyes, too, but two back eyes were elevated about four inches. I remember the fine bread and cakes she could cook on it.

Mrs. Florence Angermiller
March 14, 1938

Mrs. Arthur B. Duncan
Floydada, Floyd County

We had lived in our dugout home for seven years before Floyd County was organized, that land then being attached to Crosby County. My husband was elected the first judge of the county when it was organized and the election held. The polls were held at our dugout, and there were nineteen voters. I cooked dinner for them. I enjoyed being in "social life" again quite as much as I had enjoyed the camp meeting years ago. My son was now seven years old, and I had three daughters aged five years, three years, and fifteen months, when we moved from our dugout home into town. The town which was the county seat was first called Floyd City. It had to be changed when it was discovered that there was already a town in the state by that name, and they discussed calling it Duncanville. This, too, was ruled out because of a Post Office already in existence by that name, and they finally called it Floydada.

I cannot express the emotions I had when we moved our goods into the town and into a real house. It was only a two-room frame house, but it had real windows and doors and wooden floors. A queen in all the splendor of her palace could not have gloried in her riches as much as I did in that home. I had walked on dirt floors for so long that it took me a long time to become accustomed to hearing the sound of my footsteps on the floors, as I went back and forth at my daily work. The children, too, were bewildered and overjoyed at the change in our fortunes. They had never seen such a home before. In this "palatial" residence we lived, entertained such guests or wayfarers as came our way, and, when the county institute was held in Floydada, we even boarded some of the teachers.

Lumber for the houses and business buildings in the new town was hauled down from Childress. There was only one other residence besides ours, at first. The other people moving in lived in dugouts until they could arrange for the building of more substantial homes. The business section consisted of a hotel, two dry goods stores, and an open saloon. Court was held in the upper story of the Ainsworth Dry Goods store until a courthouse was built many months later. The first school house was a frame building about thirty feet long, and there were just about twenty-five pupils for this first school. With the coming of the railroad a few years later, more people came in and the town grew accordingly.

We felt ourselves to be quite prosperous, considering our prospects in those early days on the canyon. We had acquired twenty-four head of cattle, a wagon and a team, and our small stock of household goods. The things we had brought with us from Montague County had seen such hard usage as to have passed on in favor of newer things. It was necessary for us to reach out and take advantage of every opportunity, no matter how small, that came our way. Our family was large, and even with the changed conditions of living in a town where we had neighbors, we still put up with hardships that the present day woman would find it hard to take.

Changes came quickly. Our family grew, and we added on to our two rooms until the big old house as it stands today was completed. As the town grew we had advantages for our children far in advance of anything we had known ourselves. The new age was being ushered in. We were able to secure music lessons for our girls as they grew to school age. We owned an organ which was the pride of the household and which was considered the height of luxury in those days.

My husband, Arthur B. Duncan, was county judge of the county where he established his homestead for eighteen years. I recall the coming of R. T. Miller and his family to Floydada, where Mr. Miller served as the first county clerk of the county. Another old-timer of those first days of Floydada was J. D. Starks and his wife. They still make Floydada their home.

About two years after we moved to Floydada, my husband brought a grist mill into the town, and people for miles around would come in to have their milo maize, corn, and other grains ground into meal. This grist mill was run with the wind, and we did business when the wind blew. Sometimes my husband would get up way in the night to go grind meal for some fellow, when the wind would rise after a still day. With the passing of the mill and other contrivances of the pioneer days, came in the new era, bringing its mills, its elevators and all of the kindred machinery and equipment known to modern days for the answering of the needs of man. So must pass all pioneer days, as the years bring fulfillment of their promises to the newer generations.

Delise McGuire
July 22, 1936

CHAPTER 11
Settlers

Mrs. W. H. Downing
Wichita Falls, Wichita County

According to Mrs. Downing, the Downing Brothers' Nursery was the first nursery in Wichita Falls, and her husband built the first greenhouse there.

    I came here in 1884, starting from Fort Sill where I had been for three or four years. My father worked for the government saddle and harness shop there. We started in a government Red Cross wagon. We were with a crowd of people coming this way. We could not get across on the ferry, so we stayed all night at Grogan's. They took us on to Henrietta the next day, and we came on the train to Wichita Falls. My father worked in the harness shop of John and Henry Stockett on Ohio Avenue. The first man I spoke to was Ike Marcus.
    Mr. J.A. Kemp had a little general merchandise store in a red brick building on Ohio Avenue. We lived in a little log house on Ohio, several blocks south of the stores.
    I used to see the cowboys ride through and shoot up the town, but they didn't mean any harm; they were just having a good time.
    At that time there was just one Sunday school, and it was a Union school. Judge Barwise was superintendent. Miss Lula Barwise played the organ.
    When school started in September, we met in the little building that stood where the Masonic Temple now stands.

Chapter 11 — Settlers

As the school grew, the authorities put up another, until there were several little separate rooms on the lot.

In September, they had the first annual picnic. Barbecued beef, pickles, and light bread were served to all who came. The picnic was held on the old Williams place out on Holliday Creek. Lots of people came from nearby towns. Many of them did not come prepared to pay hack fare from the depot to the picnic grounds, and they had to walk out through the deep sand. There were no sidewalks anywhere, and the sand was several inches deep in the roads in some places. Hundreds of Indians came and that night they got together out at the Knott Barn on the hill and had a war dance.

Old man Gilbert from Gilbert Creek neighborhood used to bring milk and deliver to every one who wanted it. He had chain harness instead of leather on his old horse, and we could always hear him coming. We just hung our bucket on the fence, and when he came along he just measured a quart of milk and poured into it. He was a very kind-hearted old man. One time a widow woman was about to stop taking milk because she could not pay for it; he found it out and brought the milk without pay.

My husband, Mr. W.H. Downing, came here in 1885, and he and his brother and a man named Dud Hart started the first nursery in this part of the country. They bought a piece of land just north of the river, where they grew their nursery stock. The drought came in 1886, and they did not make anything. Their former employer at Terrell, Texas, offered them their jobs if they would come back, but they refused. During that year, carloads of flour were sent in to the drouth sufferers, but they did not accept any help.

In 1889, Mr. Downing and I were married.

The rains came and times got better, and the Downing Brothers' Nursery began to be a going concern. They bought more land south of town known as the Keen place, where the Cedar Park Pool now is located. Mr. Downing had the first greenhouse in Wichita Falls on our little home place north of the river, and people drove out from town in their buggies after flowers.

Mr. Downing and his brother had a windmill on their farm south of town, and did some irrigating on a small scale, and raised all kinds of vegetables for the market. Later when water was available from the Wichita Lake, they knew how to use it and had irrigated gardens all the time. Later Mr. Downing sold out the nursery business to his brother, and he spent his time raising strawberries, tomatoes, green peppers, etc., for the wholesale produce market. One wholesaler dubbed him "The Pepper King," for he seemed to be the only man around here who could grow sweet peppers. Each spring he raised early vegetable plants and sold them all over this vicinity.

Mr. Downing and my mother, Mrs. Bettie Gentry, organized a little Sunday school across the river in 1891. Mother went out and collected money and built a little house, which had two rooms and an L. It was made a mission Sunday school, later abandoned when so many people moved away from that side of town.

Mr. Downing was very active in the work of the Methodist church, and was Superintendent of the Sunday School for sixteen consecutive years. He was one of the earliest stewards of the church, and at the time of his death in 1926 he was the oldest steward in point of service and in point of age.

Ethel C. Dulaney
August 19, 1938

Mrs. J. W. Britt
Amarillo, Potter County

Mrs. Britt tells how her husband obtained a homestead when another man had also filed a claim for the land, and how she may have given the nickname of "Devil's Kitchen" to the Palo Duro Canyon.

Mrs. J. W. Britt, who in June, 1938, will have been in the Panhandle 49 years, is the daughter of pioneer Tennessee parents. With her parents she came to Austin, where she spent six years before coming as a wife to the High Plains of northwest Texas.

When Mrs. Britt arrived in Amarillo at midnight one hot summer night, she was met by her husband, who was boarding in the young cowtown while he plied his trade of tinner in

Chapter 11 — Settlers

the town and over the entire Panhandle.

The next morning Mr. Britt took his wife and their small son, Harry, to their new home on a section of land about two or three miles southeast of town, south of the present site of Elano cemetery. Mrs. Britt entered the pine lumber and corrugated tin-roofed shack of one room, 32 feet by 14, with the nostalgic misgivings of the housewife accustomed to finer things, but she gave no sign. This was her home. Her husband and her son were with her. That circumstance counted for more than fine furniture and painted walls.

With the instinct of the born housewife to make a home in mansion or shack, she set about arranging her household. There were not enough corners in which to put the few articles of furniture that she had. Boxes which had contained five-gallon tins of gasoline were camouflaged as kitchen cabinet, shelves, tables, and what-not. The simple pins table was surrounded with pretty hangings to hide stowaways, articles not needed and put away from unsightly prominence. Sleeping and eating, everything was done in the one room. But she soon changed all that. Taking her husband's wagon sheet, Mrs. Britt doubled the vast canvas and tacked the material to the ceiling and one side wall of the room, leaving the other side free to be used as a doorway. With an ingrain carpet on the living room floor and crisps, fresh draperies at the windows, the bare walls began to look like home.

When her husband came home from his work that evening, Mrs. Britt stood with tired, flushed but happy cheeks against the background of a miraculously transplanted home and saw the look of wonder and pride that came ever his face as he saw the difference made by a few deft touches of a woman's hand. The wagon sheet fell into place just then and shut out the envious world as he gave her a great bear-like, appreciative, home-hungry, heart-hungry hug.

Mrs. Britt, who brought the first geraniums to the plains country, placed the potted plants of assorted shapes and sizes upon a wooden frame constructed by her son, Harry. The cheerful flowers brightened still further the little home and the life within its walls.

But only for that first summer did she have to raise her little family in the dreadfully hot tin-roofed building, for soon a half-dugout reared its head proudly beside the prairie shack. Several rooms gave a greater freedom and enjoyment of home duties and home pleasures.

Behind that pioneer home lies an interesting story, which can be read in the files of the Texas Land Office and the court records in Amarillo.

When Mr. Britt applied for a land patent, after filing on the section of land later occupied by the little home, he was informed that another man had filed on the same section. The land office refused to issue a patent to the land until the two claimants had settled the question of priority between themselves.

The other contestant for the homestead was a man from Claude. Mr. Britt consulted his lawyer and the latter reminded him that possession was still nine points of the law. Accordingly, Mr. Britt gathered up lumber and some tin for roofing and went out to the site and started building a one-room shack to substantiate his claim. He had scarcely begun when he saw a strange sight which evolved into a wagon, a surrey, some lumber, and his rival coming across the plains with the same thought in view.

Mr. Britt greeted the newcomer pleasantly. There was no animosity between them. That night a terrific rainstorm came up. Mr. Britt, in the comparative comfort of his new home, which he had completed sufficiently for shelter, walked over to the other claimant and invited him to share the refuge. With no other thought than that of common hospitality, he made his guest welcome and comfortable.

Later, when the case to try title to the land came up in court, Mr. Britt's lawyer, interrogating the second claimant, asked, "Did you stay all night on the land that first night in your home or in the house of Mr. Britt?" The honest contender for the homestead rights had to answer that be had taken shelter in the home of his rival. That point cinched the case for Mr. Britt. The homestead was declared his.

On the plains, south of the section upon which the Britt home stood, many thousands of cattle from South Texas remained for weeks while they were under quarantine, forbidden to progress farther until they were disease free. Cow chips, dried to a crisp in the strong sunshine of the

Chapter 11 — Settlers

Panhandle, was sometimes gathered to be used on summer days to make a hot, quick fire. Mrs. Britt called the strange fuel very appropriately, "surface coal." However, she used coal and gasoline for her stoves for the most part. Many early settlers were glad to have herds "bed down" or stay near their homes to harvest a supply of this "prairie hay." Before the railroads came, bringing coal conveniently near, fuel was scarce an the plains. Buffalo chips and cow chips were cheap and easily obtainable.

Sometimes trail herds were held for weeks at a time near the Britt homestead. Mrs. Britt had occasion to learn the generous and considerate nature of the cowboys who tended the cattle. She found that they were not the dreadful creatures of whom she had heard so many tales "back there" in Tennessee, that they were gentlemanly, courteous, and respectful of womanhood. Frequently they would come up to the house with a quarter of beef which they had killed. Mrs. Britt has many kindly memories of those "knights who came riding."

Mrs. Britt, unlike many of the first pioneer women, had near neighbors from the very first, some living from one to two and three miles away. One of these neighbors, a very sweet woman from Iowa, could not seem to overcome her nostalgia for the trees and greater vegetation "back home." She complained to her neighbor, Mrs. Britt, that her young son had no tree under which to play. However, she became reconciled to the plains in time and learned to love them, as does everyone who comes and stays for any length of time.

Neighbors in those days were "closer" then they are today, in spite of the long distances between neighbor and neighbor. At Christmas and other holiday periods, they all gathered at the home of one or the other of a group, like relatives in other places and times. And they had great fun and pleasure together. They had good things to eat, also. Those persons who have the mistaken idea that the pioneers of the plains set scant tables would drool at the mention of juicy buffalo steaks, antelope meat cooked as only a plains housewife or range cook could prepare it, wild turkey, done to a turn, broiled quail or plover, and prairie chicken, which their predecessors enjoyed. Vegetables were supplied from gardens or from tins.

Canyons and river breaks provided wild grapes and plums and a few wild currants for jellies, conserves, and pies. No, those days were not all hardships; far from it. Mrs. Britt agrees with other pioneer women that those years were the happiest and best of her life.

One of the greatest pleasures enjoyed by friends and neighbors together was an occasional outing trip to the Palo Duro Canyon, during which they would remain for several days or weeks, reveling in the beauty of the scenery, gathering fruit, and indulging in the usual pleasures of the camp. Mrs. Britt, who recalls that fifty years have wrought great changes in the erratic course of the Palo Duro gorge, stood amazed at the picturesque panorama which spread into the distance on her first sight of the canyon.

It was on this initial visit to the Palo Duro Canyon that Mrs. Britt, upon seeing the peculiar natural formation now known as the "Devil's Kitchen", exclaimed, "Why, that must be the Devil's Kitchen!" Another member of the party, pointing to a stray piece of cloth, shouted laughingly, "And here is a part of his wife's dress."

To Mrs. Britt's knowledge, the canyon feature had not been named before this time. Ever afterward it was spoken of as the Devil's Kitchen.

Mrs. Britt lived on the homestead near the outskirts of Amarillo during the early days when the citizens were moving from Old Town. She recalls one of the devices used by the promoters of the new townsite of Amarillo to get the people to settle on their land. Passenger trains coming into Amarillo on the Denver tracks passed a siding near the new site. To induce travelers who were prospective settlers to stop in the new location, some one was prompted to announce "Amarillo" at the siding pause. Thus many unsuspecting persons got off at that point, thinking they were in the real town. This scheme also brought guests to the Amarillo Hotel on the Sanborn acreage.

Mrs. Britt was living in Amarillo when several hundred head of wild cattle, shipped in on the Fort Worth and Denver Railroad, broke through the ice on Amarillo Lake near the tracks and drowned, because they were unable to move themselves due to their weakened condition and the coating of ice.

Chapter 11 — Settlers

Their owners salvaged only the hides, which were taken from the dead animals by kindly neighbors.

At the time, Amarillo was the largest cattle shipping point in the world. Thousands of cattle were held at the prairie west of the town, awaiting shipment from the stockyards located on the site of the present zinc smelter of the American Refining Company.

Mrs. Britt remembers riding in the first passenger trains on the old Pecos Valley line to Canyon and points southwest. The passenger trains were freights with travelers riding in the caboose. She was delighted to be permitted to ride in the tower, or lookout, of the caboose which she had heretofore thought of as the throne room of the impressive "conductor" of the train.

She also recalls a humorous story about the railroad which was long in coming to Canyon. A Mr. Conner, pioneer rancher of the region, was most hopeful of the railroad's coming. Every morning he would climb the slope upon which his ranch house stood and look toward the northern horizon, folks said to see if the train's smoke were visible. "Connor's train smoke" came to be a common jest. Anything chimerical [unrealistic] was likened to "Conner's train smoke."

When Mrs. Britt first come to the plains, she was met by the sight of a vast sea of waving grass, high and lush mesquite. Grama grass seems to have been a later comer to the plains grass range. She recalls no weeds or flowers on the open plains when she first came into the region. Weeds followed the plow. She often heard the expression by early settlers, "If we could only make a weed grow."

Furrows were ploughed, Mrs. Britt recalls, about each section of land to prevent the destruction by fire of the precious range. The prairie fire was the greatest dread of the early settlers on the plains. A disastrous fire could destroy in a few minutes the pasturage for the wintering of herds and farm stock. Mrs. Britt has a theory that the stunted wild plum thickets hovering together in canyon and river breaks are a result of former great prairie fires.

Mrs. Britt was living on the outskirts of Amarillo at the time of the Indian scare of 1891. Her husband, returning late from town, told her of the wild rumors over the plains concerning an Indian attack. Jokingly, she told him, "I suppose it they had really come, you would have left us here to be scalped." However, Mr. Britt had ascertained the falsity of the report, which was spread as a practical joke, so it was said. But many men and women hurried to a central point in Amarillo for common protection, as did the inhabitants of both rural and urban districts all over the plains region at the time.

Mrs. Britt remembers Dr. Cartwright, whose wife still resides in Amarillo, as one of the first doctors in the town. Dr. McGee was another physician practicing in Amarillo in the early days. His daughter is now [in 1938] teaching at Texas Tech at Lubbock.

Mrs. Britt, with others, gathered the impression that a certain man who donated land for St. Anthony's Hospital and another building at the opposite side of town, did so with the thought of the ultimate connection of those two points by a street, which later became known as Polk.

Mrs. Britt knew the four girls who were the first graduates of an Amarillo school: Eula Trigg, now Mrs. [W. D.] Twichell; Mary Brookes; Daisy Martin, now Mrs. Tom Curry. Among early teachers in the town school were professors Witherspoon, Woodson, and Ramsey, who was the first teacher to grade the school. A man named Twichell was the first to establish a college in Amarillo. Harry Britt attended this college and one established by J. D. Hamlin, Mr. Franks, and Mr. Bryney.

Freighting at the time was done by settlers on the south plains from Amarillo, preferably, as it was nearer and the travel better, or from Colorado City, although no regular road existed between these towns and the plains.

Grass in those first days grew so high that a pony staked with an ordinary rope could not graze off all the grass in the circle enclosed by his night's pasturing.

Mrs. Britt, as do many other old-timers, recalls the harder winters and deeper snows which typified the plains weather in those early years in the Panhandle.

Mrs. C. M. Cohea
March 2, 1938

Chapter 11 — Settlers

Mrs. Belle Little
Mart, McLennan County

In 1866 my father, J. W. Mulloy, married Sarah Louise Douglass, who was the daughter of J. C. and Isabel Douglass of Springfield, Illinois. To my father and mother there were five children born; three of us were small children when they came to Texas. I am the oldest, born the 3rd of April, 1867. All have passed away but my sister, Mrs. St. Clair of Waco, and myself. The boys were Jim and Joe, both deceased, and a sister, Edna, also deceased.

We located in 1872 near the village of Bosqueville, where Father made a crop. This was only a few miles north of Waco. Father carried his produce to market at Waco, which was a small village also, but larger than Bosqueville. We attended the little Baptist church at Bosqueville.

My grandfather Douglass had already moved to Bosqueville, so to join him we made our first home at this place. However, we decided to go farther west, and in 1873 we moved to Comanche, Texas. Father had a hundred acres in wheat and it was growing fine, when in June there came a late frost and killed it. This discouraged him, and then he moved to what is the Blue Ridge settlement southeast of the town of Marlin, Texas.

We children attended the public school in Reagan and attended church at this place. Father farmed on a large scale and prospered at this place, but there were a number of families from the Blue Ridge settlement who had moved to the old Willow Springs community, now known as Mart, my grandfather Douglass among them. Others were the Harlan and Cowan families.

In the year 1878 we moved to the settlement east of Willow Springs. Mrs. Laura Cowan was my first teacher at Mart, she having taught in the term of '79 and 1880. Other families who lived in this community now known as Mart were that of Breland, Howard, Reynolds, Stodghill, and farther east was the Hardwick ranch owned by Uncle Jack Hardwick, my husband's relative.

Other teachers following Mrs. Cowan (over in the old school house and church which stood in the cemetery under the old elm tree that stood for a century, almost, and under which the Mart Baptist Church, with a membership of eight, was organized) were Mr. Westmoreland, a Mr. Cressop, McJunkin, and Hunt. When the new school house was built across the little branch which was between the cemetery and the village of Mart, there was a Mr. Bob Allen, who was a brother of Mrs. Carpenter; also Mr. W. A. Allen, Mr. Overby, Ben F. Dancer, and others at a later day.

My grandfather Douglass came to Texas from Illinois and first settled in the Bosqueville community, later moved to Reagan and then the present Mart community. He was buried in the old Salt Branch Cemetery near Marlin on Blue Ridge. He had a large family of boys, eight boys and two girls. They were Perry, Pole, Tom, Henry, John, Buck, Dick, and Jim. Uncles Perry and Pole were old enough to enlist under the flag of the Confederate states and served throughout the conflict. Perry was a sergeant of Company A, 15th Arkansas Regiment. He was born in 1842 in Illinois and died May 20, 1916, at his home in Mart.

Uncle Pole is 93 years of age and lives at his home near Mart. Uncle Tom is around 83 years of age and lives in Houston. They are the only surviving members of this family of children. There were two girls, my mother Louise and her sister Callie, both deceased. Mother passed away in September of 1916.

In 1881 I married William LaFayette Little, who came to Texas and lived with his Uncle Lum Hardwick, a brother of Captain Jack Hardwick of the Hardwick Ranch, now known as the Gillam Ranch. Mr. Little was a native of Burnsville, Mississippi, and came to Texas in 1872.

We bought our home two-and-a-half miles from Mart, in what is now know as the Elm Ridge settlement. Here we reared our family of three children. They were William Arthur, who is now acting head of the Texas Old Age Assistance Commission and lives at Austin; a daughter, Dora Dean, whom I reside with and who married John Drinkard of the Victoria settlement. The youngest son, John, is in the Federal Tax Collecting office at Houston. Mr. Little passed away April 3, 1922.

The spirit of adventure did not die out with our pioneers. My brother-in-law, Bill Johnson, whom my sister, Edna,

Chapter 11 — Settlers

married, had his share of it. He took part in the rush to the Indian Territory when it was opened by the government to the homesteaders.

He was living at Cleburne, Texas, and when the date of the opening of the Territory was set, he joined the host of people to make the grand rush....

From the experience [in the Oklahoma land rush], this brother-in-law, Bill Johnson, gained the incentive of seeking his fortunes farther west, and so in a few years he decided to try them in Mexico. He lived there for several years and accumulated a nice ranch and had a profitable stock business when the Diaz revolution came, and he was warned repeatedly to leave the state by the revolutionist. He brought his family out and left them in Texas, then returned to Mexico to try to sell or see what he could get out of his holdings, and to this day that is the last we have heard of him. We naturally felt that he had been killed by the faction which had given him warning.

When my husband's relative, Captain Jack Hardwick, first settled the Hardwick ranch (now known as the Gillam ranch), he sent for his brother whom we call Uncle Lum and who was one of the first preachers in this part of the county. While Captain Jack was herding up his cattle for the Northern markets, Uncle Lum was herding up the lost sheep of the Lord. It mattered not if some of the converts were of the clan which bore the brand of "G.T.T." (Gone to Texas), which at that time meant they had reason to leave their homes in the old states, and it was true that it was not uncommon for a man to inquire of another why he ran away from his home back in another state. And it is equally true that few people felt insulted for these questions.

Justice descended into the body of Judge Lynch, sleeping when he slept, and waking when he awoke, but gradually out of this has come with as much rapidity as could be expected the status of our law and order, from the days of Richard Coke, who took up his fight to bring it into being, to the day he was inaugurated Governor of Texas following the days of Reconstruction.

Miss Effie Cowan
n.d.

Mrs. Lizzie Powers
Marlin, Falls County,
and Mart, McLennan County

I was born in 1866 at Bedias, Texas in Grimes County. My father, Dr. George Wyche, with his family, came to Texas about the year 1859 from the state of Mississippi. He was a plantation owner and sold his plantation with the slaves and came to the new state of Texas, seeking a better climate for the health of his family.

My father was one of three brothers who left their native state. The other two were lawyers; one, James, married a Miss Bancroft from the North. They freed their slaves and moved to California and from there the state of Washington, where he became a judge. The other brother, Beverly, went to Philadelphia and became an attorney.

There were two sisters who remained in Mississippi. They were Mrs. Mary Wyche Thomas and Mrs. Fannie Wyche Morrison. Each one was a refugee; one from the siege of Vicksburg and the other from Jackson, Mississippi, when General Grant captured it. Both returned to their old home in Byrom, Mississippi. I can remember many stories told of the hardships endured during the time they were in the cities during the War Between the States.

I can also remember the stories told of their trip to Texas after the war was over, to see my father in his last illness a few years after the war closed. Especially do I remember their mode of travel by boat and by stage, how they had to wait for the Mississippi River to go down from one of its rises when they crossed the river.

During the time my father was in the army, my mother taught a little school at Bedias and rode horseback, taking her two children, Fred and sister Laura. Sister Laura later became Mrs. Laura Cowan, a pioneer of the country around Mart. My older brother, Eugene [Wyche], and sister Fannie stayed at home. Brother farmed and sister Fannie kept house. When my mother arrived at her school, they hid their horses in the thicket nearby to keep the Union soldiers from taking them as they passed on their way to Galveston to rejoin the

Chapter 11 — Settlers

Union men stationed there.

After my parents passed away, my brothers and sisters moved to Bremond. There my brothers engaged in farming, and sister Fannie married Mr. Jim Owens of the Reagan community. Sister Laura taught a little school near Bremond until she married Mr. Henry Clay Cowan, who had just come to this community from Tennessee with Mr. Owens.

I lived with my sister, Fannie Owens, for a few years, and then after my sister, Mrs. Cowan, moved to the Mart community, I lived with her until I married Mr. Sam Powers in 1883.

When my sister, Mrs. Cowan, first came to Mart, they had just begun to raise cotton. When they took it to Waco to the market, they hauled it by wagon train, a distance of twenty miles. By the time they reached Waco, it would be near the noon hour, so by the time they had marketed the cotton and bought their supplies, it was too late to make the return trip, as it took four hours, so they usually spent the night in Waco.

Mr. Cowan had a little store over where the old town of Mart was located.

In 1880, Mrs. Cowan taught the first six-months' school ever taught in Mart, in the first Baptist church, where the Mart Cemetery is now located. This was a long building made of rough box lumber with old homemade benches. All the children old enough to attend school in the whole community east of Big Creek came to this school. There were twenty-eight pupils. The name of both the school and church was Willow Springs; it was later changed to Mart.

The following families were represented in this little school—these names were taken from an old roll book kept by Mrs. Cowan. One page of the roll book is missing, and only the names of twenty-two pupils can be given: John Suttle, Daniel Suttle, Ike Suttle, Gus Douglas, Kate Douglas, A. E. Young, Daniel Young, Hattie Pevyhouse, Mamie Shelton, Clarence Stephens, George Tidwell, Tommie Douglass, Eddie Hunter, Joe Hunter, Mary Vaughan, Nora Vaughan, Watts Vaughan, Mattie Douglas, George Douglas, Annie Chancelor, George Arnold, Philip Arnold. The Suttle children were sons of the pioneer Baptist minister. Many of these and the teacher, Mrs. Cowan, have answered the last roll call.

In my sister's notebook are the names of the first ten families to settle between 1877 and 1880 at Big Creek at Willow Springs. These were Albert Breland, W. H. Criswell, Perry Douglass, Pines Shelton, W. B. Stodghill, H. C. Cowan, W. H. Francis, H. T. Vaughan, Mr. Arnold, Mr. Brooks, and a young man named Willie Easter who lived with Mr. Brooks. To the best of my knowledge, all these men have also died.

I have often thought of the difference in the country here in 1877 when my sister, Mrs. Cowan, came to this community and now. Then, this was just after the Indian depredations had ceased, the range was free and open as the crow would fly, abounding in deer, wild turkey, wild hogs and all the wild animals that lived in this country. The cattle, horses, sheep and goats grazed on the hills and prairies near the water holes, and old Willow Springs over near the cemetery was one of their favorite watering places.

In 1883, I married Sam Powers, who was a ranchman and lived ten miles northeast of Marlin, in the vicinity of Big Creek. He was a grandson of Elijah Powers, who joined the Robertson colony in Tennessee and came with General Robertson to old Nashville in 1834, where he lived for a year and then moved to East Texas, and in 1844 came to Falls County and settled on a league of land which the Mexican government gave him, when Mexico was giving the colonists land for the settling of the state.

Grandfather Powers had five sons: William, who died in Falls County; Lewis B., who took part in a number of Indian fights and died in Falls County, also; Andrew Jackson, who was killed in the Indian fight following the Marlin-Morgan Massacre [see Indian Stories].

Other sons of Grandfather Powers were Elijah and Francis, the father of my husband. Francis settled in Falls County and engaged in ranching until he enrolled in the Confederate Army. He served the duration of the war. He returned and helped in the organization of Falls County. He died in January of 1877. He reared a family of six children. His eldest son, Joe, was a stockman of Falls County who moved to Edward County, where he died. Tom, another son, moved to Archer County. My husband, Sam, lived near Mart. A daughter, Mary, married William Waite of Reagan; another son, Frank, moved to Falls County, and still another son, John, lived at Reagan. All these are deceased.

Chapter 11 — Settlers

After I married, I lived on the ranch in Falls County, which was ten miles north of Marlin. I lived there about twenty years.

About 1901, we moved to Edwards County and lived fifteen miles from Rocksprings, the nearest post office.

When our children were old enough to enter school, we returned to Central Texas, because it was fifteen miles out west to the nearest school.

Miss Effie Cowan
n.d.

Mrs. J. B. (Laurel) Mobley
Lubbock, Lubbock County

One of Mrs. Mobley's teaching jobs was tutoring the children of ranchers. After she moved to Lubbock and married, she was instrumental in getting the first church building constructed in Lubbock.

I was teaching school in Virginia when I decided to come to Texas. I always was adventurous and I said to myself, "Laurel Davis, I want to see a little of this old world." Texas seemed, in those early days, a long, long way from Virginia; still the more I contemplated the trip, the more daring I grew, so I advertised in the *Fort Worth Gazette* for a school to teach in Texas.

I got several offers and after carefully considering each one, I made up my mind to accept a position in a school at [a town in Travis County]. So in September, 1888, I left my native state and came to Texas.

My work was pleasant and I liked the country fine, though I have never considered the scenery of Texas anything comparable to that of Virginia. But I was well satisfied with my new location until my health began to fail and it soon became apparent that the climate of Travis County was not agreeing with me, so the next year I secured a school at Colorado City and came West.

The rugged beauty of the west enthralled me and I began to take positions out on the ranches as private tutor for the ranchmen's children. For several years I taught on ranches over the country, then in 1897 I came to Lubbock and taught two terms here.

In 1899 I was married to J. B. Mobley, who was at that time the Treasurer of Lubbock County. We had a very quiet wedding. Our ceremony was performed by Reverend Liff Sanders, who still lives in Lubbock. I was a Baptist and had never felt that I could have my marriage vows administered by a minister of any other denomination, and Brother Sanders was a Christian, but he was the only preacher there was in Lubbock at this time, so we asked him to read the ceremony.

We located on Singer Street, which is now Avenue H. For awhile I busied myself with the affairs of my home and the social life and educational work of our village, then one day in 1900 while I was out in the yard working with my little flowers, I got to thinking about Lubbock not having any church house. We always had our religious services at the courthouse, and I came to the conclusion that it was time to start taking up a collection to build a church house. I was wearing a big shade bonnet, and I just walked right on up town with that bonnet on.

The first man I met was George M. Hunt. When I told him what I wanted to do, he gave $10 for the church. That was the first donation on the Baptist Church; I collected $70 that afternoon. I was so elated when I went home that I took my bonnet off and waved it triumphantly as I went down the street. It seemed to me that the church house was in sight. I could just see how it would look, and I kept right on talking to people about it and asking for donations. I sat down and wrote to people who I thought would like to see a church built in Lubbock and who were able to contribute and would like to do so.

I received a hearty response from most of those whom I had solicited. C. C. Slaughter sent $50. Fuqua and Smith of Amarillo donated. J. M. Dupree of Mt. Pleasant and R. H. Lowry of Brady made donations. Then we received $100 from H. L. Kokernot of San Antonio, with a request that it be used on a parsonage for the preacher. Lester Lewis, banker of Canyon, gave $50 for this fund also.

We got a considerable sum of money. We had the money, or at least enough to make a good start, but somehow it seemed

Chapter 11 — Settlers

Courtesy Southwest Collection, Texas Tech University, Lubbock, Texas

View of Lubbock, ca. 1910.

that we just could not get the church up, and then one day I received word to "Let up on the church for awhile. We don't need a church built in Lubbock now." I sent word back, "Lubbock does need a church and I intend to keep on working for one until we get it."

It wasn't that I wanted to run things. Where I grew up in Virginia, we had old churches. In my childhood I had always gone to church, and I learned when I was quite small to take part in the services. After I came west I just couldn't go on without some form of worship. When I taught on the ranches, I used to get my Bible down an Sunday morning and read to the little children, and I taught them religious songs to sing.

It was not long after I received the request to let up on the church building that Lubbock County ranchmen came down to our house to discuss ways and means of getting the church started. This was in January 1901, and pretty soon the building was put up. These men were George M. Boles, J. W. Winn, E. Y. Lee, all of Lubbock, and R. M. Clayton, who owned ranch property in Lubbock County, but resided in San Antonio.

I have watched with great interest the building of all of the churches in Lubbock. For some time after the Baptist church was built, it was a sort of community building. We were always glad for any denomination to have their services there, when we were not [having services] ourselves.

We had a good Presbyterian meeting here in 1904. The Presbyterians did not have a church here at that time, but two Presbyterian preachers, Rev. Hammock and Rev. Anderson came to Lubbock from Colorado City to hold the meeting. They did not stay at the hotel; they brought a few quilts and a little camping outfit along with them and batched.

It so happened that at this time a house just below us was vacant, so the preachers went down there to camp. Mr. Mobley and I loaned them a feather bed, for we knew that they couldn't be very comfortable on a pallet of quilts. They had good services, and we all enjoyed them so much.

On Saturday we asked the preachers to take dinner at our house. We had plenty of young frying chickens then and if I do tell it myself, I used to be complimented on making extra good salt-rising bread. We had an excellent meal,

and the preachers talked over their work in the meeting and planned the services for the next day. Brother Hammock asked me if I would supply them with some salt-rising bread to use in their Communion services. Of course, I was glad to do what I could in religious work and I readily agreed to provide the bread.

But they did not get to have the Communion services the next day. It came the biggest rain that night that I think I ever saw in my life. Lubbock did not have any drainage system then, and water stood everywhere all over town. When we got up the next morning and looked down at the house where the preachers were camped, we knew that they could not get out and cook their breakfast on a camp fire, so I hurried and fixed up a basket of hot food for them, and Mr. Mobley put his old high-top boots on and waded down to the house and carried the basket to them. Later in the day, when the clouds had drifted away and the water had run off a little, we looked out of a window and saw the Reverend Anderson splashing up the muddy road, coming to our house, bringing the feather

Chapter 11 — Settlers

bed home on his back. The rain had broken up the meeting and the preachers were preparing to go home. Shortly after this one of the Presbyterian brethren arrived in his wagon and helped the visiting preachers load up their camping outfit, and they left Lubbock.

I have been on the Plains for [41?] years. I have been happy here, and I have thrilled with the satisfaction of seeing Lubbock progress and grow from a few houses on the prairie to an enterprising little city. I feel that both my husband and I have helped to make Lubbock what it is today, but now he is gone, and I can no longer take active part in the things that go on about me, so I just sit here and think and think.

Sometimes I pass the time away writing. I used to write almost incessantly when I was in Richmond College in Virginia. After I started to teaching school, I did not have so much time to write, but even then I wrote for a long time for *The Blue Ridge Echo* in Little Washington. Later I was a correspondent on the staff of a South Carolina paper. After I came to Texas, I gradually put my writing aside, but after Mr. Mobley died I became almost a shut-in following an accident and subsequent ill health. I turned to my writing again to help me through the lonely hours. Since then I have written several articles for some of our leading magazines, and also some historical and geographical items for the *Dallas News*. But writing tires me now, and so sometimes I just sit and think of my childhood home in the shadows of the Blue Ridge Mountains in old Virginia where the mountain laurels grow. That is why my parents named me Laurel, because the laurels grew all around our house and Father loved them so. After I started to school people began to call me Laura, but Father never did.

Virginia seems far, far away indeed now, much farther than Texas seemed to me in these early years. All of my relatives are still in Virginia, and now I am alone on the Great South Plains. Of course, I have friends, for whom I am very thankful, and I have my memories, the most pleasant of which are the early years of my marriage, the years when the plains was still a cattle country and Lubbock was only a village trying to build schools and churches.

Ivey G. Warren
December 28, 1936

CHAPTER 12
Historic Towns

Mrs. George R. Bean
Estacado, Crosby County, and Lubbock, Lubbock County

Estacado was the first county seat of Crosby County and seemed to have a good future. It boasted a courthouse, several stores, a boarding house, and the Central Plains Academy, established by Quakers who lived there.

My father, Dr. William Hunt, was a physician employed by the government in the Indian Territory, for 10 years. I was born 25 miles south of Arkansas City in the northern part of Oklahoma, but my parents moved to the South Plains when I was quite small and located at Estacado in 1881.

The land around Estacado used to belong to the State of Texas, but Paris Cox acquired part of it and started a little settlement there. This settlement was generally known as "The Quaker Colony" and was the only Quaker settlement ever established in the state of Texas. In 1884 the population was estimated at 100 inhabitants, numbers of new families moving in each year, so that at times it seemed that Estacado would grow into a nice little town.

There was one church in the colony, the "Friend's Church." They had a frame building where they conducted their services. Also, we had a school there; this was the first school on the plains and is often spoken of as the first school in Lubbock County, but it was really not in Lubbock County. It

Chapter 12 — Historic Towns

was in Crosby County; however, Crosby County had not as this time been organized.

My sister, Emily Hunt, was the teacher in this first school on the plains. She taught in a dugout and had only six pupils, and I was one of the six. I am afraid I did not apply myself very diligently to my books, though I was only about five years old, and as my sister was the teacher I felt privileged to do as I pleased.

There was only one water well in Estacado at this time. It was called "The Public Well," and was dug by Paris Cox, who hauled the rock from Blanco Canyon to wall the well.

The plains suffered a drouth in '84, and the people had to buy almost everything they needed. The stores had to have their supplies hauled from Amarillo and Colorado City, in that they sometimes ran short on provisions. Rice corn was the principal grain crop raised, and when they continued to face a shortage on flour, rice corn was ground into meal and this was used to make hoe cakes. We had plenty of rain the next year and raised abundant crops.

There was one thing that was a great help to the little settlement during the lean years, though, and that was that there was nearly always plenty of meat for the tables, for wild hogs were still to be found in the country, and thousands of antelope and buffalo roamed the plains. There were a good many deer here then, too, and these provided food for a good many of the people. A number of the colonists raised small crops; some of these were cultivated with wild horses which they captured between Estacado and Amarillo. These animals soon became domesticated and learned to do the work of the ordinary work horse on the farms.

Estacado enjoyed a year or two of prosperity and was on a building boom when the county was organized. The county seat was located at Estacado, and they built a jail and a two-story courthouse there. A number of new residences were erected, and we already had a boarding house, "The Llano House," which was owned and operated by my father's cousin, George M. Hunt. Cousin George also had a store. There was another store which was owned by Charlie (Hokins?).

The Central Plains Academy was established in Estacado by the Quakers during this time. J. M. Moore of North Carolina was one of the teachers [Editor's Note: This probably refers to Jesse H. Moore who was head of the Academy]. However, Estacado was not to continue her forward march into a prosperous town, for the county seat was moved to Emma. Later it was located at Crosbyton. The Central Plains Academy closed after about two years, as so many of the Quakers left Estacado that the enrollment was not sufficient to keep the school open, so it was discontinued.

We left Estacado and came to Lubbock to make our home in 1893. We already had friends and relatives in the new town, and though it had at this time just a few houses set out here on the big, wide, prairie, we found it a wonderful place to live, and in all these years I have never changed my mind, I have watched Lubbock grow; I have done what I could to help it grow. We have had drouths and sandstorms, and in 1893 we had a grasshopper plague; the grasshoppers even ate the grass in the pastures that year. But all the way around, I think the plains is the best place in the world to live.

I am often amused at some of the fictitious tales about our early days here. I presume that imaginative minds, lacking the real facts upon which to base their stories, simply elaborate to fill in and make up a yarn. The result has been in most instances merely ludicrous; however, there have been some misrepresentations made which have been deeply resented by the pioneers, because they were utterly untrue.

There has been one report circulated to the effect that the Quakers at Estacado used to give dances for the Indians. I am sure that this is not true. I grew up at Estacado; the people there were relatives and friends of ours, and I most certainly never had known or heard of anything of this kind to have happened. In the first place, the Quakers did not dance themselves; neither did they give dances. Besides that, the Indians had been vanquished from the plains before the Quaker Colony was established at Estacado. I remember hearing of two groups of Indians passing through the settlement, but they only camped overnight and went on their way, so that with the exception of a few who straggled through the country now and then, we did not have them in our midst, and the colonists would not have associated with them had they been there. The Quakers did not dislike the Indians, but it is preposterous to assume that the Quakers would have had any entertainments for them, whatsoever, had they been in the settlement. The Quakers, it must be remembered, where a very religious sect, and their socials were always conducted in a strictly dignified manner.

I recall my two sisters' wedding ceremonies back in 1884, while we were living at Estacado. The Quakers' marriage ceremony was indeed a very solemn ritual. My sister, Emily, was wedded to A. A. Anson, and my sister, Susie, to C. L. Swarts. The Quaker preacher, Anson Cox, performed their ceremonies. My sisters have both lived in the state of Kansas for a number of years, and about three years ago they went on a trip together, way up into Idaho. There they unexpectedly met up with Anson Cox. They wrote me that he was getting to be a very old man now. Anson Cox was a cousin of Paris Cox, the founder of Estacado.

I think that the young people enjoyed themselves much better in the days when I was young, than they do now. We did not think it was necessary to debase our morals in order to have a good time, either. The old folk took part in things in those days. We had singings, debates, and community suppers, socials of that kind in which my father was always a leader. He enjoyed life and we had a happy home, though we had some hardships and had no conveniences or comforts in those days, such as we have in the present time, yet we had the things that are really worthwhile. We had love and happiness in our home, and we had good friends. We always had some books and magazines to read, which were exchanged with neighbors. People used to share their pleasures and their sorrows together in those early days on the plains.

Ivey G. Warren
n.d.

Mrs. W. M. Anderson
Durango, Falls County

Mrs. Anderson rode on the first train that came to Dallas. She was living in Hunt County then, but moved shortly to Durango in Falls County.

I was eighty-six years old on the 11th day of March, 1938. I came to Durango from Hunt County with my husband in 1873. It was just a short time after the railroad came to Dallas, near our home, and I can recall its coming. It was an occasion for celebrating when the first train came into Dallas. A big crowd assembled at the depot, and when the train stopped, a group of gay young ladies climbed on the train. When the bell rang and the whistle blew for it to start, the conductor tried to get us to get off the train, but we girls just stood waving and stayed right on the train and had our first train ride on the first train into Dallas.

We arrived in Durango about the time the white people had the last encounter with the Indians. There was a band who were captured at Gatesville for stealing horses, and several Indians were caught and a white man who was thought to be the leader.

We made our first two crops before we saw barb-wire. Brush fences and rails were used. Our farm was part of the land formerly owned by Joe Jackson. Of course, we had livestock of our own, but ofttimes in those days we bought beef and never asked questions as to where it came from. We had the idea many times that we were eating meat that had been stolen and sold to us, but there was nothing we could do about it.

Money was desirable but more of a curiosity, and we often resorted to resourcefulness in getting what we wanted by trading. Mr. Anderson went into trade negotiations whereupon the three mules and horse which brought us here were exchanged for 28 acres of timber land along Deer Creek.

The family stretched a tent in which we lived for ten months, our nearest neighbor being three miles away. We then started grabbing the timber, and when the land was cleared we planted corn and cotton. We kept warm in the winter and cooked on an open fire at the mouth of the tent.

Between times, Mr. Anderson cut logs and hewed boards with which to build our home. Our first crop was made with one work animal and the use of a neighbor's horse, which we borrowed. In six years' time, we had saved enough outside of our living expenses to buy a sewing machine and have biscuits to eat on Sundays, once in a while, which were a great luxury.

Sometimes fortune was not so kind, and we had failures in our corn crops, and then we had to dig down into our savings and buy it. I can remember when corn cost $1.10 a bushel.

For our clothes, we spun the wool to make thread for knitting socks and stockings and suits and dresses, and dyed the thread with copperas or pecan bark.

There was not a public school near our home, and our children were first taught in a room of our home. When the weather got warm in the spring and summer, the men built a brush arbor joining our house for the pupils, which by that time had embraced the near neighbors. Plank boxes were used for desks, and there were eight pupils at one time. As time went by and Durango became a village, there was a school there, and our children went in a cart, a distance of five miles, carrying their lunch for themselves and the horse.

Moscow was the first post office in this section. It was located in a field on the farm of (Lerrell?) Jackson, known today as the Sam Hart farm. The next post office was West Falls, not far from the old Carolina cemetery. It was moved from there to the present site of Durango, and with the coming of the rural routes, it was discontinued, and the inhabitants received their mail from Lott, Texas.

Lee Farmer, whose family has been identified with the settlement since the seventies, claims that Dodson Wells was known before Durango. These wells were watering places for the travelers on the pioneer trail which connected Marlin and Belton, county seats of Falls and Bell counties. Many travelers camped at these wells for the night, when on their journeys through this section.

One of the earliest mail carriers was J. P. Weathers. His

route was from Marlin to Belton, and he often had to swim the river on his horse. He had many and varied experiences. Later, when a Waco-to-Cameron road was laid out, it crossed the Marlin-Belton road north and slightly westward. Naturally the post office was more convenient at the crossroads.

Automatically the spot became known as West Falls and the post office went there. For a long time it was known under this name, but later it became known as Durango. The town was a thriving business place until the coming of the San Antonio and Aransas Pass railroad which brought the towns of Lott, Chilton, and Rosebud into existence. It was then that many businessmen moved to these other towns.

As late as 1892, Durango was a thriving settlement of 250 inhabitants. An old directory reveals that the following were engaged in business and professions at that time: W. H. Barnes, contractor; R. R. Boyd, teacher; Davis and Anderson, grocers; J. C. Dulaney, druggist; A. E. Ellis, blacksmith; S. Forenander, contractor; J. W. and W. A. Henslee, merchants; G. E. Hocutt, Methodist minister; A. R. Joyce, grocer; J. S. Llewellyn, physician; T. J. Laughlin, postmaster; J. L. Russell, teacher; Stuart and Cox, dry goods; J. D. Storey, blacksmith; and R. B. Whitesides, physician.

In succeeding years, Durango dwindled, as many of its inhabitants moved to the towns located on the railroad's only seven miles, leaving only a farming community and a people devoted to good citizenship, instead of the thriving business center it once was—where stores and workshops helped to keep the town alive and where the first West Falls County newspaper was published.

This story would not be complete without mentioning the names of the first settlers of the Durango community. Long before the Civil War, the Jackson family settled near Deer Creek, not far from where Durango is today. Another pioneer who came before the Civil War was Uncle George Storey. His house stands today. He was a blacksmith and made ploughs and wagons for people all over the country. Over near where Chilton is today, the Weathers, Coxes, Landrums, Gardners, and Wrights lived. Uncle Bruce Storey, Uncle Ben Bouchillion, and Mr. White came after the Civil War from Alabama and settled near where the town of Durango stands. I mentioned

Mr. Weathers carrying the mail during the war, and because he was carrying it for the Confederates he failed to receive any pay.

Mr. Dodson settled on his farm among the first settlers near Dodson's Wells, which were used to furnish water for the community. Others who came to the Durango settlement right after the Civil War were the Llewellyns, Farmers, Stewarts, and Uncle Drive Currie. Mrs. Cox was a long-time resident of Durango. She died only a few years ago. She had a good mind to the last and often related historical incidents. She was personally acquainted with Gen. Sam Houston.

Another settlement which played a historic role near us was the old Carolina settlement, located on the site of what is now the Carolina cemetery and church, all deserted except these two landmarks. This community was so closely related to Durango in its pioneers and their activities that it may rightfully be considered the progenitor of Durango. If the history of Durango were carried back to the fifties, it would lead to old Carolina. The earliest pioneers west of the Brazos River settled along the sandy-loam ridge upon which Carolina sprang up first as a center of activity, then Durango. A church was built about 1853 at Carolina, and it is supposed that the same building was used for a school.

It is generally conceded that the same building used for the school was also used for the Presbyterian church, and as far as history goes, the first Presbyterian church that came into existence west of the Brazos river. In the upper story of this building, a Masonic lodge was organized, but it was finally moved to Chilton, where it is in existence yet.

It was on the 12th day of October that the Carolina Presbyterian Church was organized, with eleven members and two ruling elders, namely, A. V. Lee and J. Hobbs, and Rev. J. T. Black. The organization took place at the home of A. V. Lee on Elm Creek, five miles from Cameron. This church was first named Elm Creek, but as most of the members, soon after, declined to move to Deer Creek in Falls county, it seems that the name was changed to Deer Creek, before the organization was reported to the Presbytery.

The name was changed to Carolina in October 1864. A young man named A. B. Frazier was appointed clerk of the session, but it does not appear that he was an elder. He was drowned soon after in Elm Creek. Rev. L. Tenney took charge of the church in the fall of 1854 and was installed as pastor in April of 1856, by the Presbytery, which held its spring meeting then, and this relation continued until the end of 1859.

The first church building was erected in 1859, built of lumber sawed by Mrs. Lea's sons, by hand. Later a church was created in 1883 and dedicated in 1884, H. C. Smith preaching the sermon. Mr. Balch preached for the church several times and ordained the elders chosen in 1854. L. Tenney preached to the church most of the time from '63 until '68 and again supplied from '71 to '75.

Rev. S. A. King was S. S. during 1868 and J. A. Walker in 1870; R. M. Longhridge from 1876 to 1880; J. F. Paxton in 1881 to 1890; S. W. Mitchell, 1890 and '91; S. J. McMurry, 1892-'93; J. M. Cochran from Oct. some time uncertain. The above figures were taken from *History of the Presbytery of Central Texas*, by Rev. L. Tenney, who took charge as I have stated of the Presbyterian church at Old Carolina in 1854, and installed as pastor in 1856.

Total number of communicants enrolled was 154, as against the number enrolled in 1895, as being 48. This decline in enrollment in 1895 shows the effects of the passing of the railroad east of Carolina. Today it is known as one of Falls County's most well-known cemeteries. Graves mark the resting place of many pioneers who [wrought?] in western Falls County. A small church still stands nearby, but it is seldom used. The communicants of this church are now listed on the rosters of other churches.

If the real story of Durango and Carolina could be brought to light, with the struggles of its pioneer families, it would be an inspiration to the younger generation. These two settlements occupy as unique and important a place in the history of Falls County as does Blue Ridge on the eastern section. Both communities wrought indelibly in history, yet the spirit of these pioneers were modest.

Most of the oldest settlers can recall vividly the untiring work of the country doctors as they rode horseback over the muddy roads in the winter and were always ready for the most [?] call. Chief among these was Dr. John Llewellyn,

Chapter 12 — Historic Towns

father of the late attorney, Nat Llewellyn of Marlin; Dr. S. P. Rice, father of the late Dr. S. P. Rice of Marlin; and Dr. R. B. Whitesides, who lives at Lott today.

I failed to mention another organization which came into existence during the heyday of Old Carolina, which was the United Friends of Temperance. This is revealed in ancient minutes of that organization in possession of Mrs. Annie Poulson of Lott, Texas. This organization flourished in the 1870s, and the roster of its membership is a glimpse into the early families of Carolina and Durango.

The charter members were W. E. Jackson, Joe Lea, Hugh Lee, Ben Freeman, Tilman Busby, Jesse Hedrick, Milton McLain, Bud Peters, James Snodgrass, Sam Jackson, Dick McCullough, and the following Sister of the organization, Kate Lea. Sue Wright, Ida Freeman, Annie Wright, and George Bonner. Other members who joined this order soon after formation were J.S. Johnson, Joe Honeycutt, LaFayette Hood, J. W. Storey, S. Crump. W. A. Cook, Miss Annie Wright, Mamie Harwell, S. E. Peters, Tom Gaither, Millie Gaines, Charner De Graffenreid. L. H. Hall, Forrest Gaither, James Gaither, Ed Lane, John Edge, John English, J. H. Bone, Lida McCutcheon, T. B. Garland, Miss Josephine Daffin, Mrs. Mary Gaither, I.R. Richard, and many others I do not recall.

Jesse Hedrick, charter member and recording secretary of the United Friends of Temperance, lived at Durango when it was a thriving community and was publisher of a newspaper known as "The Durango Enterprise." He was justice of the peace at Durango, county commissioner and deputy sheriff of Falls County at different times.

In 1919 my husband, W. M. Anderson, died. Eleven children were born to us, five of whom are now living. They are Mrs. Mary Gardner of Durango, Mrs. Lois B. Marshall of Marlin, Mrs. Joe Waite and Gillis Anderson, both of Durango, and Captain Charles Anderson of San Antonio. I may claim to be the sole survivor of the first families which came to the Durango, Carolina settlement in the early days.

On the 11th day of March, 1938, I celebrated my eighty-sixth birthday at my home a half-mile west of the Durango-Bell Falls Road, where the school and church is located.

Yes, I have seen lots of things that have happened in the

early days of this community. There's much I love about Falls County. Of course, I've experienced disappointments and heartaches, and for many years was not satisfied about leaving Hunt County in 1873. I felt that perhaps we should have stayed there, but our destiny brought us here. I've lived a long and comparatively happy life and am ready for the call Over There to the Great Beyond.

Miss Effie Cowan
n.d.

Mrs. Lucinda Permien Holze
Industry, Austin County, and Riesel, McLennan County

A village named Industry, near Brenham, was home to Mrs. Holze for many years. Her husband operated a country store there and later owned another store at Stamps. Mrs. Holze was living at Riesel at the time of the interview.

I was born in the year 1857 in Mechlenburg, Germany. My father, Ludwig Permien, emigrated to America in the year 1871. He settled at the town of Fredericksburg, Texas. When he was located, he sent for my folks in the year 1873. By this time he had become a naturalized American citizen. The War Between the States was over and the worst of the Reconstruction days were past, but there were still some Indians in the western part of the state where we came.

The country was mostly a stock and ranch country, but in between the hills there was timber, and so they raised their grain in these valleys. When they took their stock and produce to the markets, they went to San Antonio, Austin, and Brownsville. There was lots of Mexicans near our town, and the German settlers employed them to clear the brush from the land they put in cultivation and to help herd the cattle. There were very few slaves at this time in Gillespie County. The settlers lived in log cabins, and the schools and churches also were the log houses.

The schools were the one-teacher schools, and the teachers would board around with the families of their pupils, and the salaries were around twenty-five dollars a month. After I was grown, I went to Austin and helped do housework for the white women. Then in 1879 I married Mr. Frederick Holze and moved near the town of Brenham, Texas, to a little village named Industry.

For many years my husband operated a little country store at this place. I have heard him tell about when he was a sixteen-year-old boy during the Civil War, how he was a teamster and drove the freight wagons from Industry to Brenham and on down to the nearest railroad. The wagon trains would go together to protect each other from the robbers. Sometimes when they were passing through the river bottom, the robbers would take their wagons with the freight and the teams. The men would be glad to escape with their lives.

I can remember when I lived in Austin, how the Rangers would be stationed over on the Concho River to watch for the Indians. They were still giving trouble, robbing the settlers of their stock and their grain. I can also remember the old courthouse in Austin. It was located down near the Colorado River. The course of the river ran through the city, making a very picturesque picture with its large trees that bordered the banks of the river.

When the river was on a rise, we crossed on the ferry boats, and when it was low it was easy to ford, as the bed of the river was rock. Sometimes in the spring, it would get on a big rise and overflow the lowlands near the city. The people who lived in these places would have to move to higher ground. It was about the time I left Austin in 1879 that they built the new capitol.

After I came to Industry, near Brenham, I was surprised to see such large farms. They called them plantations. They were situated close to the rivers, the Brazos and Little River, and many were called the Bottom plantations. The soil was very rich, and they often made a bale of cotton to the acre. There were so many more Negroes. They had been slaves of the plantation owners, and since their freedom they were working the land for their former owners, and the owners were giving them part of the crops for their work.

A Legacy of Words — Texas Women's Stories 1850-1920

The towns of Brenham and Industry are near Little River, as well as the Brazos, and sometimes it overflowed, too. The Santa Fe Railroad would be under water and the trains delayed for days at a time. The white people lived away from the bottom, but the Negro cabins were down on these plantations, and it was common for the white people to have to go and bring them out in boats when the overflows occurred.

In 1884 my husband brought his family to the German settlement near what is now Perry, Texas. We owned a little store and he was postmaster at a little place called Stamps.

It was at this place that we had our experience with robbers. One afternoon as we were ready to close the store, two men rode up on horseback, came in and asked for tobacco. As my husband turned to get it, they drew a gun on him and told him to give them all the money he had. At the same time, the other one turned to me and told me that if I made a noise that he would shoot me. Then he turned to help the man who held the gun on my husband, rob the cash drawer and safe. When he did this, I ran to a neighbor's and gave the alarm, but when the neighbor got there they had the money and were gone. We never did recover of our money or find the robbers.

I will not attempt to give you the story of the German settlement at Perry, but there was a young man from Germany by the name of Von Holwegg, who was among the colony that Mr. Schlimbech brought over. This young Holwegg accumulated a large amount of property and made Mr. Otto Rau his overseer. Mr. Rau also was one of the first ones to come over from Germany with this colony. My son, Louis, married his daughter, and after Mr. Rau died he took charge of this property and is the agent yet.

I have five living children. They are Mrs. L.H. Schmidt of Riesel, with whom I make my home; Mr. Louis Holze, Waco; Mr. E.J. Holze, Otto, Texas; and a daughter, Mrs. A.L. Leifeste of Houston, Texas. My husband passed away in 1918 at the age of sixty-nine years.

I can give you a little of the history of the early days of some of the German communities in Texas before the Civil War came, as handed down to the descendents of those who were among the first settlers. It is said that in the spring of 1846 the first train for Fredericksburg, consisting of twenty wagons and some two-wheel Mexican carts, left the town of New Braunfels for the new settlement on the Pedernales [River]. There were about 120 men, women, and children in this train, accompanied by eight of the soldiers furnished by the Society for the Protection of German Immigrants in Texas.

After a trip lasting sixteen days, they arrived at the future town of Fredericksburg. It is worthy of note that the meat for the first meal served to them in this new location was bear meat. John Schmidt, one of the military soldiers, shot a bear on the banks of the Pedernales River.

The immigrants passed a band of Indians just before they crossed the river, and when they heard the shot from the rifle, they thought it was an Indian attack, but it was only the hunters shooting at the bear. Another soldier killed a panther just before they crossed the river; the timber here was dense and the animals were plentiful.

A partial list of the first settlers has been kept, but the full list seems to have been lost since the county clerk's records were destroyed by fire in 1850. Among the family names are Ahelger, Schmidt, Lochte, Bonn, Berbens, Schwars, Strackbein, Durst, Syeubing, Heinmann, Llein, Leydendecker, Eckhardt, Neffendorf, Theile, Schneider, Fritz, Weidenfeld, and Schnautz.

It is a matter of record that the first school in Fredericksburg was organized by the Society for the Protection of German Immigrants in Texas. John Leydendecker held the school in the church building. When the first city school was organized in 1856, August Siemering was chosen as the teacher. By 1860 there were ten schools in the settlement around Fredericksburg and an enrollment of 260 pupils. In 1860 the number of white people in the country was around twenty-seven hundred, thirty-three slaves and thirty-eight people in business.

The first religious service for the German immigrants was held in the city of Houston in December 1839, and in a short while there were regular services held for them in the city by a Mr. Ervendberg, who came to Houston from Illinois in 1839. In the years 1840 to 1844, this Mr. Ervendberg and Mr. Johann Anton Fisher organized Protestant churches in Industry, Cat Springs, Biegel, La Grange and Columbus. The Catholics also had churches in New Braunfels and Fredericksburg. The first mass was celebrated in New Braunfels by a priest named George Menzel, who in the same year built a cross on the Kreutzberg Mountain, to the northwest of Fredericksburg, to show to the world the Catholic standard as a symbol of salvation and civilization.

The first Methodist church organized in Fredericksburg was in the year 1849, and Rev. Eduard Schneider organized it and held the services in the Society's hall until 1855, when the congregation built a churchhouse for themselves.

On the eve of *Whitsuntide*, the Germans of Industry and Cat Springs organized a German order under the leadership of Friederich Ernst, which was to further immigration and correspondence between Germany and Texas and to preserve the German traits. To belong to this order, the requisites were talent, ability, and education. In March 1843 the members showed their patriotism of Texas by celebrating the anniversary of Texas Independence. After this there were organized various clubs and societies for the social life of the communities.

In telling of the social life of the German people of that day, my story would not be complete without telling you of the invisible passenger that came with these first families and that was the talent for music as expressed both with instruments and in song. To the march across the wilderness of this state, it accompanied them and helped them to win in their struggles against the hardships of the life of the pioneer.

The first singing society in Texas was organized at New Braunfels in March 1850. It was called the "Germania." Some of its first directors were Petmecky, C.F. Blum, Dr. Adolf Douai, and H. Guenther.

Besides the Germania, two other clubs were organized at New Braunfels before 1861. One was a chorus of men and women, and one was called the "Concordia." There was a quartette at Sisterdale composed of men, and at Comfort there was a quartette composed of Ernst Altgelt, Fritz Goldbeck, C. W. Boerner, and Fritz Holekamp under the direction of Hermann Schimmelpfennig.

In August 1853 there was a state song festival (Staats-Saengerfest) with the above-mentioned singing societies taking part together with others from San Antonio and Austin.

There were four other state meetings before 1861 at New Braunfels and Fredericksburg, but when the Civil War was declared, then the song festivals were ended for the duration of the war.

The culture of the pioneer German people was also manifested in the art of painting, and what wonderful colors to draw their inspiration from. In the spring the landscape was brilliant with the wild flowers, the bluebonnet, the Indian blanket with its coat of red, and the "Yellow Rose of Texas," the song the Confederate soldiers loved so well to march by, as well as many other flowers of equal beauty.

Hermann Lungkwitz was one of the most prominent of the landscape painters. His scene of Bear Mountain near Fredericksburg, the Pedernales River, Marble Falls on the Colorado, and Waller Creek at Austin are among his best work.

Two of Lungkwitz's paintings hang on the walls of the south entrance hall of the State Capitol Building. One is that of David Crockett, and the other shows the surrender of Santa Anna to Gen. Sam Houston. The portraits to these paintings were done by the artist Huddle, but the landscapes are the works of Hermann Lungkwitz.

The success of the German settlements in Texas is due to a great extent to the Society for the Protection of German Immigrants in Texas. The immigrants came to Texas to escape oppression in their country and to enjoy the blessings of liberty and the rights of citizenship. This they accomplished, and at the same time their ways, customs, and characteristics were preserved.

Miss Effie Cowan
n.d.

Mrs. Ernestine Weiss Faudie
Indianola, Calhoun County, and Riesel, McLennan County

Before and after the Civil War, Indianola, in Calhoun County, was an important port on the Texas Gulf Coast. A flood in 1875 and a hurricane in 1886 caused the town to be abandoned.

I was born in Dembaw Province, Possen, Germany. My father was named Frederich Weiss, and followed his ancestor, Louis Weiss, who came with the colony that settled at Fredericksburg, Texas. My father settled near Brenham, Texas, in the year 1853, the year that I was born, as I was a five-month-old infant when they left Germany.

There were farms and ranches where they settled, and over at the colony of Fredericksburg there was quite a little town. I have the list of names of the men who were in business; among them was Louis Weiss, who was a tinner. The records show that thirty-eight men operated ten different types of industrial business in the town. This town and New Braunfels were the main German settlements when my father came to Texas in 1853. The Germans around Brenham had drifted from these places to other settlements.

To the colony at Brenham my father came, and this is where I was raised. We had the ordinary little schools, and the teachers were mostly the one-teacher schools. They were paid very little, but then it was something to even have a school. So it is not surprising that the young people married early and raised their families in large numbers, to what they do now.

I was seventeen when I married William Hamburg. We came to the little settlement called Sandy Creek where the town of Riesel is today, but at that time there was nothing but ranches and the farms over near the Brazos River.

We lived there for a few years and the grasshoppers came and ate up our crops, so we moved back to Brenham and lived there for twelve years. Then in 1890 we came back to this part of the country and lived at the Perry settlement until late years.

I reared nine children by my first husband. They are Mrs. John Scharlach, who has lived by the Methodist Church in the Myers settlement on the Mart-Waco Road for the past forty years; Mrs. Fred Witting of Perry, deceased; Mrs. Louis Bohmfalk, whose husband was a Methodist minister, now deceased; Mrs. Arthur Grebe of Mart; William Hamburg and Albert, of Dallas; Mrs. Ida Busse and another son, Fred, of Baton Rouge, Louisiana.

My first husband died in 1900, and in 1905 I married

Chapter 12 — Historic Towns

Judge J. Faudie who is living with me now.

There was a grist mill close by our place, and they ground the meal real fine and crushed it and called it flour; anyway, we made our light bread out of this ground and crushed corn. We cooked over a fireplace with a big dutch oven. We spun and wove the cotton thread to make our clothes.

When we first came to this country, we lived in a log cabin, but we had it made good and comfortable and we did not mind that. We were so happy to have all the land that we could cultivate and the stock which was so plentiful, so different from where we lived in Germany. When the war, which they called the Civil War, came, I remember that my brother-in-law, Henry Hamburg, did not want to fight, as he did not believe in war, and so he went to Mexico and then up to the North where he stayed until the war was over.

My family came to the Perry settlement in 1890, and there was a big ranch called the Stone Ranch. They had lots of cattle and horses, and the cowboys would round up the cattle twice a year and take them to the markets. I think they took them to Houston or Galveston and shipped them by way of the Gulf to New York and the foreign markets. We lived in the Schlimbech settlement. The community was thinly settled, but we were a settlement of people from the old country and we kept up our interest through the papers in the old country and our way of living, also our mother tongue, and so we did not feel so isolated from Germany, although we became naturalized American citizens soon after coming to this country.

I will tell you the story of the Indianola flood that came in 1875. My brother-in-law who did not go to the war, Henry Hamburg, came back when it was over and became a Methodist minister. Most of the churches were either Lutheran or Methodist then. He was in charge of the Methodist church at this place when the big storm came. He and his wife both were drowned and most of the inhabitants. At that time and during the Civil War, Indianola was an important port of Texas, and it meant to Texas what Galveston does to us now.

There were just a few of the buildings left when the storm was over. A few feet of the outside wall was all that remained of the once big department store of Lichenstein's and Alexander's. After the flood, Mrs. Lichenstein moved to

Corpus Christi and went into business. The courthouse, which in those days was at least fifty or sixty feet from the bay, has later been washed almost entirely away by the water of Matagorda Bay. It is said that the walls of these two buildings, a few crumbling cement cisterns, and a few old safes that were in the store is all that is left as a reminder of the once second most important port of Texas.

The story of Indianola reads like a story book for children. They claim that La Salle was the first to make a camp there, while he was trying to find the mouth of the Mississippi River. However, it was made the county seat of Calhoun County in 1846. Many of the buildings and underground cisterns were made of concrete, so this is why those the storm left stood. It was said that the stage left twice a week for California, and the prairie schooners carried the overland freight and the Morgan Line steamers were used for passengers and freight by water.

Another story is that gold and silver bullion was brought from Chihuahua, Mexico, for shipment to the mint at New Orleans. Instead of the horses and carriages, the ox-wagons were familiar sights on the streets of this little coast town. It is said that hides and tallow were among the more important commodities. After the cattle were killed and skinned, the carcasses were hauled beyond the city limits and dumped, and the fresh beef was used for fattening hogs. The people in the town were welcome to all the meat they wanted at the slaughter house.

Natural ice from New England was shipped by steamer from Boston, army goods were shipped from Baltimore through Indianola to the forts at El Paso and San Antonio. The number of people in the town in 1875 were close to 3,500, and town lots sold for a good price, so the town was one of the best in Texas until Sept. 16, 1875, when the tropical storm came. The citizens hurried to the business buildings and private houses that were known to be the stoutest, but only a few escaped with their lives.

It was said that many were forced out of the second stories when the water rose in them, and had to seek safety in hastily constructed rafts which they made from the sections of the floors and walls of the houses they were in.

Chapter 12 — Historic Towns

Some of them were thoughtful enough to have ropes, and they were lashed to the rafts by them, but many were drowned when the buildings they were in collapsed and the people were crushed or drowned.

There were many stories of heroism that were told by those who were saved. They told about the two prisoners named William Taylor and Joe Blackburn, who were both up for first-degree murder. They had been placed in the courthouse, and during the height of the storm both frequently swam through the courthouse windows to rescue some drowning person. After the storm was over, desolation met the eye everywhere. My brother-in-law, his family, and his home had disappeared and were never seen again, although my husband hoped for months to hear of him.

Most of those who lived through this storm moved away to escape another like fate. When the second hurricane come in 1886 and was said to be of even greater intensity, the few people who were left read the signs in time to evacuate the town, and the havoc was not as destructive to the lives of the inhabitants.

After the storm of 1886, the old port of Indianola was abandoned. I have told you this true story of the coastal storms to show you what the old pioneers had to contend with, not only the pests of the insects on their crops, or the hardships of the lack of the comforts of life, but the very elements of nature, the drouths, the floods, and the unsettled condition of the country, even to desperadoes and murderers, but never for an instant did we lose our faith in the future which was always before us, to look into when the time should come when we could lie down to our sleep and not feel that any calamity would befall us.

And now in my old age, I look back over the past from the time that I can remember, and think of the many friends and kinsman who came over here from the old country, and who have passed on to the far away land, and I say in my heart to them all: *Auf Wiedersehen* (till we meet again)!

Miss Effie Cowan
n.d.

Mrs. Amelia Steward Christoffer
Mart, McLennan County

Mrs. Christoffer lived in the communities of Kirk and Victoria before moving to Mart.

I was born in the province of Possen, Prussia (which was later a part of Germany) in the year 1850. I lived with my parents at this place until I came to Texas with some immigrants from Prussia when I was twenty years of age. We came in a sailboat, and we were from March until in May on the trip. I found work on reaching the Texas port of Galveston, and in the year 1872 my father and his family came and joined me in Galveston.

In January 1873, I married Rhiner Christoffer, who was on the same boat that I came over on and whom I later met, but did not know him before I left the old country. We lived four years in Galveston, then moved to Texas City and lived nine years. We were engaged there in farming and livestock business, and when we sent our produce to Galveston to the market, we took it in a sail boat. Everybody had their sailboats just like they have their automobiles now. There were only two German families in Texas City, but we were happy in our new country and had the future to look forward to.

We moved to the community where I now live about the year [?], and came by way of Houston, then by way of Hempstead through the Navasota River bottom, through the old towns of Marquez and Groesbeck and the Tehuacana Hills, which was the home of the Tehuacana Indians in the early days of Texas. Thence on to the prairie country between the towns of Groesbeck and Waco. The community we moved to was called the Kirk and Victoria communities.

We settled on the Brown ranch, and my husband looked after it for Mr. Brown until it was divided into farms and sold. We bought our farm from him and just stayed on to the present day. The country was thinly settled, and our houses were poor and open. We went to Waco and Groesbeck for our supplies. At first we did not raise any cotton, just grain and fruit, vegetables, and our livestock.

Chapter 12 — Historic Towns

Before this ranch was cut up into farms, Mr. Brown had red barns all over it to keep his feed for his stock in the winter when the grass was gone. Then we had better houses to live in, also.

When the round-ups on the ranch were on, it took all the men on the ranch and sometimes from the adjoining ranches. They would take two or three days to get the herd rounded up, and then they had to be held together until they were driven to the train to be shipped to the market up north. The cowboys would ride around the herd day and night, and to keep the herd quiet they would sing the cowboy songs. This had a soothing effect on the herds, and they seldom had a stampede. When the herd became frightened, this was when they would stampede and run in every direction, then the round-up was all to do over again.

The Texas grass was in abundance, and the range was sufficient for the cattle until the winter months. The prairie was beautiful in the spring with its coat of wild flowers, such as we had never seen before, and the life on the ranch was full of interest and excitement as we had plenty to keep us busy. I am reminded of the cowboy song of the "Grass of Uncle Sam":

"Now people of the eastern towns, it's little that you know,

About the western prairies, where the beef you eat does grow;

Where the horses they run wild, with the mountain sheep and ram;

And the cowboy sleeps contented, on the grass of Uncle Sam."

When they had the last round-up on the Brown ranch, Mr. Brown, who lived in Calvert, Texas, came up to see to it. There were between a thousand and fifteen hundred head of cattle. This was in the spring of 1894. Most of the men in the community helped in this last roundup. Mr. Brown stayed until they were loaded on the train at Groesbeck to be shipped up North, then he went to his home in Calvert and committed suicide. Whether it was despondency over the last of the herd being gone or whether he was sick, no one knew. It was a shock to the whole community.

After this his son, Bob, came to look after the business

until it was sold off into farms. This was about the year 1896. To the north, extending clear across, was the Smyth ranch, which belonged to the father of the Smyth brothers, Alva, Lee, Dr. Tom, and Dr. Ed. The first two are deceased, but the latter ones still are living. Dr. Ed lives in Mart. There were several girls in this family, also. They first lived at Old Springfield, but later moved to Mexia. Most of this ranch is still owned by the Smyth family.

Some of the first settlers of this community, now known as the Victoria community, with their families were: W. R. Williams, Cave Johnson. Other names of the first families were Boman, Kahler, Hardwick, Vickers, Drinkard, Dyer, and Fogity. Some of the first ministers were: Baptist, Brother Jennings and Tatum. The Methodists were Lemmon, McLaughlin, Moon, Maxwell. The names of the first teachers were Adkins, Adams, McJunkin, Laird. This was at Kirk school, where we first sent our children to school.

Later on, the Victoria school was organized, and Miss Ollie Pearce was the first teacher. Then the Victoria church was organized, and Brother Tatum and Grundy were the first Baptist ministers. Brothers Moon and Davis the first Methodist ministers.

There was a preacher named Parker whom they called a Campbellite in those days. Now the name of this church is called the Church of Christ. All of you, I'm sure, understand the difference mostly is in the music in their way of carrying on their services. They do not believe in any musical instruments and try to carry on their services as near like the apostles in the Bible days as they could. This man held some very successful meetings.

We began to raise cotton in the year 1886 on the prairie. The people thought at first that it would not grow on the prairies, and so for years the section where the cotton was raised in this country was in the bottoms near the rivers. We first tried the small patches and as they did well, we then planted larger acreage. We took it to Kirk and Prairie Hill to be ginned. Tom Johnson had a gin at Kirk and a Mr. Lampkin at Prairie Hill. The first gin at Victoria was built by Henry Blake and John Mitchell. This was built on the Morgan Coker place, but was later moved to its present site, near my home.

Chapter 12 — Historic Towns

When the men had to go to court, they went to Groesbeck in Limestone County, a distance of twenty miles. One of the judges who was on the bench so long was Judge Kirvin, who afterward went to Congress. Then there was Judge Cobb, who was so solemn that it was said he was never known to smile.

One of the first doctors who came to the Kirk and Victoria communities was Dr. Briscoe, who served us long and faithfully.

My husband died in 1902. We had eight children; one, Fred, is now deceased. Those living are Lizzie, Annie, Rhiner, Katie, Betty, Lillie, Oscar. Fred married Vida Deadman; Lizzie married Wiley Mitchell and lives in the old home location. Annie married Elmer Deadman and lives at Lamesa, Texas. Betty married Steve Collins, who is the secretary of the Mart Chamber of Commerce at Mart. Lillie married Ernest Vickers; Katie married Charlie Mitchell and lives at the town of Dawson, Texas. Oscar became a doctor, married a Miss Kelly and is practicing medicine at Mexia. Rhiner has never married and has remained with me and cared for me since the death of my husband in 1902.

It is a long way back to the days of my girlhood in Prussia and dreaming of the new country "America." The reality is better than the dream; I am rich in the blessing of my home and family. This has become my own country, but it does not mean that I have forgotten the other country or the other friends and relatives.

Miss Effie Cowan
n.d.

Mrs. Phoebe Arnett
Stranger, Falls County

The daughter of pioneers who came to Texas in an oxen-drawn wagon, Phoebe Sommerville married Hansford Arnett in 1866 and settled in Stranger, a community about 15 miles south of present-day Mart. She recalls many people and events in Texas history.

I was born in Robertson County on the 30th day of July, 1848. My parents were Mark and Polly Sommerville. They came to Texas when it was under the rule of Mexico and settled near the present town of Old Wheelock. They lived with the Wheelocks and a few other families in a fort the first two years. This was for protection against the Indians.

This community was a small settlement situated near the town of Franklin in Robertson County. Most of these settlers came from Tennessee with Sterling Robertson (for whom Robertson County was named). I was 13 years old when the War Between the States started, and can remember when it was declared and the Southern states seceded from the Union. There was a company formed at Wheelock known as the Wheelock Company. I do not remember the other name, what company it was, but I do remember that I had a cousin who went with this company to fight for the Southern cause, or the cause of the Confederacy, and out of this company of 100 men, only five lived to return.

There was a drought in Texas this year, and only two men in the community raised any corn. The flour was shipped in by wagon train to the little store at Wheelock, and we had to pay an enormous price for it. We lived out in the country after leaving the fort and attended the old Shiloh church.

When my parents came to Texas, they did not have any team but oxen, and so they drove them to their wagon. This made the travel slow and they were weeks getting to the Wheelock fort.

On the 10th day of January, 1866, I married Hansford Arnett, who had returned the year before from the service in the Confederate army. He fought in several battles, some in Missouri and some in other places, but he came through it with only a bullet wound in his arm. He passed away in 1879.

We had six children, all living but one. Those living are Mrs. Mollie Tate, near Marlin; Mrs. Lizzie Richardson, who lives with me; Mrs. Edna Hays, Stranger; Tom Arnett, Groesbeck; and Robert Arnett, Kosse.

I have lived within five miles of Stranger ever since I married in 1866. I have seen the surrounding towns grow from small communities to villages and then towns. I have seen the soldiers as they passed through Wheelock as they were going and coming from fighting for the Confederate cause. We lived on the road which ran through Wheelock to San Antonio, and also to Houston. When the soldiers passed, they would often stop and command my mother to cook them something to eat. If the women did not feed them, they helped themselves to whatever they could find, such as groceries, meat, hogs, or chickens, or cattle. They considered they were fighting for us and it was our place to feed them. Very few of the folks refused to give them what they asked for.

I have lived through the trying days of Texas during the Reconstruction period, following the days of the War Between the States; the Spanish-American War, and World War I, but the most trying things that we had were the days of Reconstruction and the Indians. The delegates to the first Reconstruction Convention were elected just two days before I was married, and on a month from the day I was married, the convention met and was organized.

I came to the Stranger community with my husband when we married, in 1866. We traded at Bremond, the nearest town at that time of any size. Marlin, over about eleven miles to the west, was just a small village, as was Kosse to the east. This was long before the Houston and Texas Railroad built through Kosse. To the north about fifteen miles was the little community in later years called Willow Springs, but now the town of Mart. This community sprang up about the year 1870, I think. I know that a few of the pioneers from the Ridge moved to the Willow Springs community. Among them the Douglases, the Harlans, Jones, Cowans, and others I do not remember.

And now let me go back in memory to the early days of the Ridge, as the Stranger community was called. The Ridge takes its name from a long strip of land from a point near Steele's or Garrett's place near Limestone County and extends in a southwesterly direction almost to the Robertson County line. It is in reality a ridge, and the Stranger community lies on top of an elevated section from which one can look over a large section of the Big Creek valley westward to the courthouse at Marlin, even to Bean's Hill which is the beginning of the Brazos.

Many of the pioneers have passed on, but there are a few of us who lived in the days I have mentioned, following the War Between the States.

As we stand on the Ridge and gaze westward, eastward, northward, and southward, our minds go back to the days of the past, and once more we see in memory those others who helped to build the community. We see many horses and rigs of all sorts. The roads are winding, rough, and full of mud holes in the rainy season. In the summer they are dusty and bumpy.

The stage coach at first passes by on its way to Marlin and the east to Kosse. There is no hurry; everyone has plenty of time. We see once more the aristocratic Jasper Garrett, moving among his family and his neighbors, taking great pride in his family, his neighbors, and his friends. Once again Harris Kay conducts Sunday School in the old church-schoolhouse, or they open their home to the community for a Christmas party. We can hear in memory the chuckling voice of Arch Hodge and his quiet humor, and the voice of Mrs. Hodge in her quiet matronly way.

Then in memory one can see Jesse Brothers as he rides around his farm, watching his men at work. Then it grows dark and one can see the hounds on the run. From the woods down the ravine from the Ridge, one can hear the baying of the dogs on the chase. Following the dogs are Uncle Billy Brothers; Joe Sandlin, our humorist; some of the Erskines and the Garrets and some of the then-younger generation. They are having a great time when hunting was real sport, and at the end of the chase they brought home the deer or the wild turkey.

Around the corner of the road, near the schoolhouse and church, are the family of Jim Swinnea. And in the house are Ida and Lil and Floyd, and perhaps some neighbors passing the time of day. Ida and Lil are living in that house today. A little farther to the south and west sits John Eddins in his home. He is smoking a pipe; his face is covered with long whiskers, the style of the day, and he is meditating over the days gone by, perhaps in the service of the Lost Cause. It's warm, and in the house one can hear the hum of the sewing machine as Grandma Eddins sings, "There's not a friend like the lowly Jesus: No not one—no n-o-t o-n-e."

Once again I see beyond the old well on the south side of the road near Stranger store, just below the hills, a horse and buggy and in it sits a gentleman with an expression of peace with the world. He has a peg-leg, and he lets the horse have its way over the road. It is the mail carrier—Joel Roberts carrying the mail—and he's been carrying it since Stranger got its post office and a name.

Along the pages of memory there goes Dewitt Stone—still having a good time. He has just found a skeleton from an old Indian mound, and here comes a candidate for office, whereupon Dewitt lifts up the skull, and from thence hurriedly goes the candidate without waiting to ask him for his vote.

Then there goes young Dr. Poindexter in his buggy of bygone days, and once again we hear him tell the story of his first patient. For a whole month the new doctor hadn't had a patient and he didn't see how he was to pay his board bill at Granny Williams'. About sundown he gets a call, and all night long his patient lay groaning, grown pale, then hot, and pains in his side. The doctor tries all his remedies; it seems his patient is going to die in spite of all his efforts. He goes out to the hen-house and rolls up a big pill and gives to the patient. Immediately he relaxes and falls into a peaceful sleep from which, when he awakes the next morning, the pain is gone and he is a well man, or at least for that time, the trouble being what was later known as an attack of appendicitis, but at that time it was just plain indigestion.

Later Dr. Poindexter spent many years of his successful career practicing medicine in Kosse, serving his old-time friends at Stranger.

Riding the winding roads, a herd of cattle ahead, we see many of Strangers' fathers and grandfathers with their riding boots astride of horses, rounding up the cattle. There are bridles and harness for the buggies, surries, wagons with spring seats, and fine teams of horses and mules. Such were the modes of travel, and when the new machines called automobiles come in, we hear these fathers and grandfathers saying "You won't catch me in one of those contraptions!"

Again down memory lane we see the neighbors meeting for a big picnic among the trees in Garrett's pasture—plenty of well-filled baskets—a string band and all-day speaking, for it is election year. The band is made up of country musicians from all sections of the county. It sounded so good, despite frequent discordant notes or misplaced key. There's a lull in the enthusiasm; things are beginning to drag. The band leader knows the remedy. Shaking his fist and bringing his hand down briskly, out comes loud and clear the strains of "Dixie" and the crowd responds with the chorus of "I wish I wuz in de lan' of cotton, ole times dar am not forgotten, hurray, hurray, in Dixie lan' I takes my stan' to lib an' die in Dixie."

A sudden gleam shines in the eyes of Jasper Garrett, John Eddins, George Barnes, Jesse Cornelison, Bill Clawson, Ed Vann, Dr. Shaw, and other old Confed's, including Dave Boyles of Reagan, later Judge Boyles. The spirit of "Dixie" is catching; sons and daughters, grandsons and granddaughters alike join in the chorus of hurrahs, and there's new life in the crowd after the band plays "Dixie." The platform is cleared for an old-time square dance.

Another look into memory's pages and we see the old schoolhouse and church building which served for both, during the week for school, and on Sundays the different denominations took their turn about holding services. It is a school day and Mr. J. A. Dunkam is teaching school. There are big boys and little boys, big girls and little girls, and today these boys and girls are fathers and mothers of the younger generation. Professor Dunkam has passed on, after having led a successful teaching career and afterward made a success as a banker and farmer in the Marlin community.

But look, there are other teachers who pass on the stage of life's memory and leave their footprints on the sands of time. There is John Lattimore, whose father was a teacher, too. Professor Stout Blair and others. All took their turn in the old church and schoolhouse combined.

Then comes the Sunday services. One incident stands out clearly in my mind. The Baptists are having services. Throughout the audience, the deacons are passing the plate around with the "bread and wine" for communion. Down near the rear of the church is a young man who has imbibed of the wine of the grapes a little too freely. He rises and remarks "I want some of that!" The deacon returns "You can't have it. You're not a Baptist." He comes back with "Well, I'm a Methodist. Besides, this church belongs to us all." The deacon replied, "It may be your church, but this is our day, our time

Chapter 12 — Historic Towns

to hold service." It was then that the argument grew stronger and stronger, until there sprang up two factions: one for, the other against "Close Communion," and the outcome was the Baptists built their own church in the year 1902.

Following the long procession down memory lane comes "Granny Moffett," quiet, kindly, old-timey, typical of the pioneer women of the time she lived and spent her youth. Typical of the days of San Jacinto. She could tell you lots of things about the days when Texas was fighting for her freedom from Mexico. She ran with the other settlers in the Runaway Scrape as people fled from Santa Anna, before General Sam Houston turned the State's destiny at San Jacinto. She could tell all about when Texas won her independence and also the days of the Reconstruction, when Texas also won her independence all over again, and her fight for the vote after the men who were soldiers during the War Between the States had the vote taken from them. She saw the transformation from a Republic to a state.

This reminds me that in the month of February, after I was married in January of 1866, that the Reconstruction convention met and was organized, with Throckmorton for President, and did not adjourn until April, and at a general election the constitution was adopted and the legislature met at Austin. On the 13th day of August, Throckmorton was inaugurated Governor and Wash Jones, Lieutenant Governor. It was in March of the next year, 1867, that Congress was displeased with President Johnson's plan of reconstruction and declared the governments of Texas and Louisiana provisional only. In April of 1867, General Griffin, the military commander at Galveston, prohibited all elections in Texas. Then on the 17th day of April, he put the Negroes on the juries, with an order issued preparing for the registration of the voters. The best of my memory, the voting strength was about equal, around 56,000 whites to 47,500 Negroes.

Looking down memory lane, there unfolds a panorama of Texas history with the incidents politically, socially, and economically that have made Texas what it is today, but the picture that I like the best is the simple life of neighborliness and the companionship of the pioneers as they met in social gatherings, church, schools, all-day singings, picnics, celebrations, and in some years, the political meetings.

Entertainment came from fellowship, conversation, music, and stunts for the young. Instead of picture shows on fine Sunday afternoons, the young men and women rode their horses, played and enjoyed the simple sports. Unlike today, where the young people go to the movies and to the professional entertainments with no contact with their neighbors.

Yes, things are different. The old Ridge itself is the same. The birds still sing merrily as they fly from tree to tree, just as they did in the [eighteen] fifties and sixties when I married and came to the Ridge. The old Big Creek flows or stands still, just as in the days gone by. It is we who are different, and we are different because the progress of civilization has made us so.

Miss Effie Cowan
n.d.

Names of Women Included in This Book

Anderson, Mrs. W. M.
Arnett, Mrs. Phoebe
Bean, Mrs. George R.
Britt, Mrs. J. W.
Brown, Mrs. T. C.
Chestnut, Mrs. H. E.
Christoffer, Mrs. Amelia Steward
Cox, Mrs. Ella
Davenport, Mrs. Emily Kelly
Downing, Mr. W. H.
Duggan, Mrs. Arthur P.
Duncan, Mrs. Arthur B.
Ervin, Mrs. Eleanor
Faudie, Mrs. Ernestine Weiss
Foote, Miss Gula B.
Fowler, Mrs. George
Holze, Mrs. Lucinda Permien
Hoover, Mrs. Laura
Jackson, Mrs. C. F.
Jones, Mrs. George W.

Kemp, Mrs. J. A.
Ketchum, Mrs. Helen
Landis, Mrs. C. G.
Little, Mrs. Belle
Mather, Miss Mattie (Babe)
Miles, Mrs. Mary Leakey
Mitchell, Mrs. Frank
Mobley, Mrs. J. B. (Laurel)
Nunn, Mrs. G. J.
Powers, Mrs. Lizzie
Randal, Mrs. Fayette
Roe, Mrs. Elizabeth
Russell, Mrs. Cicero
Rylee, Mrs. J. D.
Sanford, Becky
Shaw, Mrs. Annie
Vance, Mrs. Hattie
Ward, Mrs. Mary Jane
White, Mrs. A. E.
Willis, Mrs. M. B.
Wolffarth, Mrs. George C.

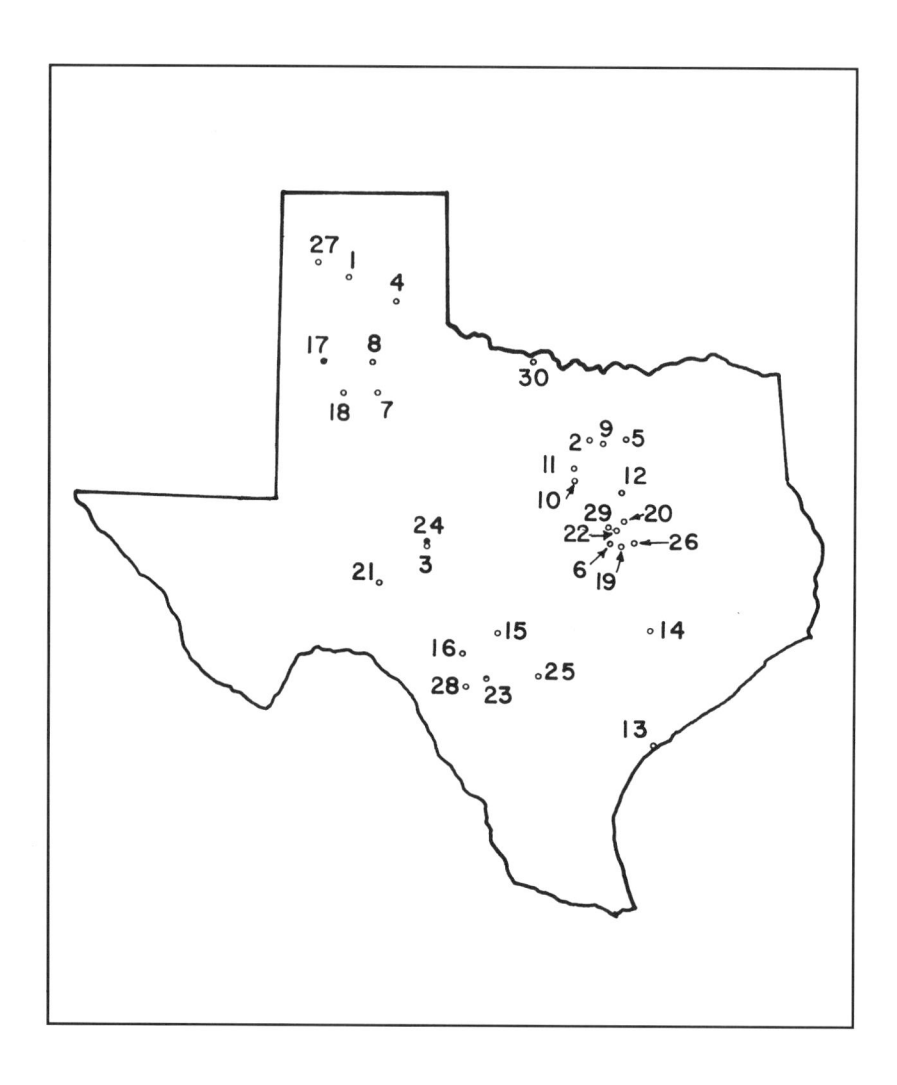

A Legacy of Words — Texas Women's Stories 1850-1920

Location of Principal Cities and Towns Mentioned in Stories

Numbers refer to map on opposite page

1. Amarillo, Potter County
2. Azle, Tarrant County
3. Ben Ficklin, Tom Green County
4. Clarendon, Donley County
5. Dallas, Dallas County
6. Durango, Falls County
7. Estacado, Crosby County
8. Floydada, Floyd County
9. Fort Worth, Tarrant County
10. Glen Rose, Somervell County
11. Granbury, Hood County
12. Hillsboro, Hill County
13. Indianola, Calhoun County
14. Industry, Austin County
15. Kerrville, Kerr County
16. Leakey, Real County
17. Littlefield, Lamb County
18. Lubbock, Lubbock County
19. Marlin, Falls County
20. Mart, McLennan County
21. Ozona, Crockett County
22. Riesel, McLennan County
23. Sabinal, Uvalde County
24. San Angelo, Tom Green County
25. San Antonio, Bexar County
26. Stranger, Falls County
27. Tascosa, Oldham County
28. Uvalde, Uvalde County
29. Waco, McLennan County
30. Wichita Falls, Wichita County

Additional Reading

Banks, Ann, ed. First-person America. New York: Knopf, 1980.

Brewer, Jeutonne. The Federal Writers' Project: A Bibliography. Metuchen, N.J.: Scarecrow Press, 1994.

Brown, Lorin W.; Briggs, Charles L.; and Weigle, Marta. Hispano Folklife of New Mexico: The Lorin W. Brown Federal Writers' Project Manuscript. Albuquerque: The University of New Mexico Press, 1978.

Couch, William T., ed. These Are Our Lives. Chapel Hill: The University of North Carolina Press, 1939.

Handbook of Texas. Austin: Texas State Historical Association, 1952. 2 vols. and Supplement, Vol. 3, 1976.

Howell, Donna Wyant, comp. I Was a Slave: True Life Stories told by former American Slaves in the 1930's. Washington, D.C.: American Legacy Books, 1995-.

Lanning, Jim, and Lanning, Judy, eds. Texas Cowboys: Memories of the Early Days. College Station: Texas A&M University, 1984.

Mangione, Jerre. The Dream and the Deal: The Federal Writers' Project 1935-1943. Boston: Little, Brown, 1972.

New Handbook of Texas. Austin: Texas State Historical Association, 1996. 6 vols.

Survey of Federal Writers' Project Manuscript Holdings in State Depositories. Washington, D.C.: American Historical Association, 1985.

Terrill, Tom E. and Hirsch, Jerrold, eds. Such As Us: Southern Voices of the Thirties. Chapel Hill: The University of North Carolina Press, 1978.

Index

Allen, Bob; 124
Allen, W.A.; 124
Altgelt, Ernst; 148
Amarillo, Texas; 5, 16, 27, 116
Anderson, Arch; 63
Anderson, Charles; 143
Anderson, Gillis; 143
Anderson, Mrs. W.M.; 26, 32, 138
Anson, A.A.; 137
Arnett, Hansford; 157
Arnett, Mrs. Phoebe; 157
Arnett, Robert; 158
Arnett, Tom; 158
Austin, Texas; 5, 77, 116, 124, 145, 149, 163
Azle, Texas; 18, 49, 57, 75
Baldwin, Henry; 37
Baldwin, M/M Moses; 13
Barnard, Charles; 68
Barnes, George; 162
Barnes, W.H.; 140
Barwise, Judge; 114
Barwise, Miss Lula; 114
Bates, Finis; 40
Bean, Mrs. George R.; 134
Ben Ficklin, Texas; 27, 41, 67, 80
Black, Rev. J.T.; 141
Blackburn, Joe; 153
Blair, Stout; 162
Blake, Henry; 156
Blum, C.F.; 148
Boerner, C.W.; 148
Bohmfalk, Mrs. Louis; 150
Boles, George M.; 131
Bone, J.H.; 143
Bonner, George; 143
Booth, John Wilkes; 40
Bouchillion, Ben; 140
Boyd, R.R.; 140
Boyles, Dave; 162

Breland, Albert; 128
Britt, Harry; 117, 122
Britt, Mrs. J.W.; 116
Brookes, Mary; 122
Brothers, Billy; 160
Brothers, Jesse; 160
Brown, Bob; 155
Brown, Mrs. T. C.; 17
Browning, Morris & Mary; 6-7
Bryan, Capt. Benjamin; 74
Buchanan, Miss Laura; 7
Burleson, John; 65
Busby, Tilman; 143
Busse, Mrs. Ida; 150
Caldwell, Molly Hayes; 15
Cantrell women; 49
Carolina, Texas; 139, 141, 143
Cavassoo, Juana; 70
Chancelor, Annie; 127
Chestnut, Mrs. H.E.; 16
Chilton, Fred; 44
Christoffer, Amelia Steward; 32, 154
Christoffer, Rhiner; 154
Clarendon, Texas; 5, 17, 38, 94
Clark, Addison R.; 7
Clawson, Bill; 162
Clayton, R.M.; 131
Cochran, J.M.; 142
Cochran, Tom; 40, 45
Coker, Morgan; 156
Collins, John; 19
Collins, Steve; 157
Cook, W.A.; 143
Cornelison, Jesse; 162
Corrigon, Miss Celia; 37
Cowan, Henry Clay (H.C.); 11, 127, 128
Cowan, Mrs. Laura; 11, 123, 126
Cox, Anson; 137

Cox, James Monroe; 2
Cox, Mrs. Ella; 2
Cox, Paris; 134-137
Crump, S.; 143
Criswell, W.H.; 128
Currie, Drive; 141
Curry, Mrs. Tom; 122
Daffin, Josephine; 143
Dallas, Texas; 4, 138
Dancer, Ben F.; 124
Davenport, Emily Kelly; 35, 72, 83, 109
Davenport, John; 85, 109
Davenport, Rollie; 92, 110
Davis, Laurel; 129
Day, J.J.; 102
Day, Mattie; 103
De Graffenreid, Charner; 143
Deadman, Elmer; 157
Deadman, Vida; 157
Dillard, George & Sarah; 110
Douai, Dr. Adolf; 148
Douglas family; 127
Douglass, Buck; 22
Douglass, Isabel; 123
Douglass, J. C.; 123
Douglass, Perry; 124, 128
Douglass, Pole; 124
Douglass, Sarah Louise; 123
Douglass, Tommie; 127
Dove Creek; 61
Downing, Mrs. W.H.; 29, 114
Drinkard, Dora & John; 124
Duggan, Mrs. Arthur P.; 4
Dulaney, J.C.; 140
Duncan, Mrs. Arthur B.; 94, 111
Duncan, Wood; 100
Dunkam, J.A.; 162
Dupree, J.M.; 130
Durango, Texas; 26, 32, 138
Easter, Willie; 128
Eddins, John; 160, 162
Edge, John; 143
Ellis, A.E.; 140

Ellis, W.J.; 82
English, John; 143
Ernst, Friederich; 148
Ervin, Mrs. Eleanor; 41
Estacado, Texas; 37, 134
Farmer, Bessie; 26
Farmer, Lee; 26, 139
Farr, Jim, Ranch; 78
Faudie, Ernestine Weiss; 53, 149
Faudie, Judge J.; 151
Fisher, Johann Anton; 147
Fisher, Mrs. Ethel; 12
Fletcher, William; 18
Floydada, Texas; 94, 111
Fly, Dr. David; 6
Foote, C.D.; 81
Foote, Gula B.; 81
Foote, Harry; 82
Forenander, S.; 140
Fort Concho; 2-3, 19
Fort Worth, Texas; 8, 22, 129
Foster, Frank; 9
Fowler, Joe; 20
Fowler, Mrs. George; 46
Francis, W. H.; 128
Fredericksburg, Texas; 12, 144, 146-150
Freeman, Ben; 143
Freeman, Ida; 143
Fuqua, W. H.; 28
Gaines, Millie; 143
Gaither, Forrest; 143
Gaither, James; 143
Gaither, Mary; 143
Gaither, Tom; 143
Gardner, Mary; 143
Garland, T.B.; 143
Garrett, Jasper; 160, 162
Gentry, Mrs. Betty; 116
Gholson, Sam; 64
Gillam, Dr. J.R.; 10
Gipson, Mrs. Irene; 12
Glen Rose, Texas; 45, 67
Goldbeck, Fritz; 148

Index

Goodnight, Col. Charles; 5-9
Granbury, Texas; 40, 67, 80
Grebe, Mrs. Arthur; 150
Green, Perry; 14
Guenther, H.; 148
Hall, L.H.; 143
Hamburg, Albert; 150
Hamburg, Fred; 150
Hamburg, Henry; 151
Hamburg, William; 150
Hamlin, J.D.; 122
Hardwick, Jack; 123-125
Hardwick, Lum; 124-125
Harper, Charley; 110
Hart, Dud; 115
Hart, Sam; 139
Hartsfield, Millage; 55
Hartsfield, William; 9, 55
Harwell, Mamie; 143
Hays, Mrs. Edna; 158
Hedrick, Jesse; 143
Henslee, J.W. & W.A.; 140
Herring, Bill; 7
Hewin, Ward; 12
Hillsboro, Texas; 1
Hobbs, J.; 141
Hocutt, G.E.; 140
Hodge, Arch; 160
Holekamp, Fritz; 148
Holze, E. J.; 146
Holze, Frederick; 145
Holze, Louis; 146
Holze, Lucinda Permien; 144
Honeycutt, Joe; 143
Hood, LaFayette; 143
Hoover, Mrs. Laura; 31, 43, 75, 79
Houston, Texas; 53, 124, 146, 147
Howard, J.W.; 12
Howard, Mrs. J. W.; 55
Hunt, Dr. J.W.; 39
Hunt, Dr. William; 134
Hunt, Emily; 135
Hunt, George M.; 37, 130, 135
Hunt, Myrtle; 38

Hunter family; 127
Hunter, Capt. Willis; 49
Indianola, Texas; 53, 149
Industry, Texas; 144
Jackson, Joe; 25, 138
Jackson, Mrs. C.F.; 25
Jackson, Sam; 143
Jackson, W.E.; 143
James boys; 40, 42
Johnson, Bill; 124
Johnson, Cave; 156
Johnson, Edna; 124
Johnson, J.S.; 143
Johnson, Tom; 156
Jones & Plummer Trail; 38
Jones, Mrs. George W.; 50, 59
Joyce, A.R.; 140
Kay, Harris; 160
Kelly, Chris; 84
Kelly, Jack; 84
Kemp, J.A.; 62, 114
Kemp, Mrs. J.A.; 62
Kemp, Syble; 63
Kerrville, Texas; 2, 93
Ketchum outlaws; 44
Ketchum, J. Van; 64
Ketchum, Jim; 64
Ketchum, Mrs. Helen; 64
Ketchum, Tom; 40, 41, 64
King, Ed; 44
King, Rev. S.A.; 142
Kokernot, H.L.; 130
Landis, Mrs. C.G.; 27
Lane, Ed; 143
Lattimore, John; 162
Laughlin, T.J.; 140
Lea, Joe; 143
Lea, Kate; 143
Leakey, Texas; 47, 71, 105
Leakey, John; 105
Leakey, Mattie; 107
Leakey, Tom; 107
Lee, A.V.; 141
Lee, E.Y.; 131

Lee, Hugh; 143
Leifeste, Mrs. A.L.; 146
Leonard, Mrs. Van; 103
Lewis, Lester; 130
Leydendecker, John; 147
Little, Arthur; 21
Little, Belle; 21, 30, 52, 61, 123
Little, Dora; 21, 124
Little, John; 124
Little, Wm. Arthur; 124
Little, Wm. LaFayette; 124
Littlefield, Texas; 4, 23
Llewellyn, Dr. John; 142
Llewellyn, J.S.; 140
Llewellyn, Nat; 143
Longhridge, R.M.; 142
Lowry, R.H.; 130
Lubbock, Texas; 25, 37, 129, 134
Lungkwitz, Hermann; 149
MacGregor, Mrs. Bertha; 7
Magruder, Gen. John B.; 53
Marcus, Ike; 114
Maria, Jose; 74
Marlin, Texas; 46, 53, 74, 93, 123, 126
Marlin-Morgan Massacre; 74
Marshall, Lois B.; 143
Mart, Texas; 9, 21, 30, 32, 46, 52, 53, 54, 61, 74, 93, 123, 126, 154
Martin, Daisy; 122
Martin, Mrs. James; 12
Mather, Ada; 78
Mather, Mattie (Babe); 47, 75, 77
Maxwell, Zack; 102
Mayer, Mrs. Newton; 63
McCrohan, Eugene; 64
McCullough, Dick; 143
McCutcheon, Lida; 143
McDonald, Jack; 70
McDonald, William; 67
McFadden, David; 50, 59
McFadden, John; 50
McIlhany, Dr. Marshall; 7

McLain, Milton; 143
McLennan, Neil; 61
McMurry, S.J.; 142
Menzel, George; 148
Miles, Albert; 108
Miles, Jonathan; 42
Miles, Mary Leakey; 47, 71, 105
Miller, Earnest (Dusty); 18
Miller, R.T.; 113
Mitchell, Charlie; 157
Mitchell, John; 156
Mitchell, Mrs. Frank; 44
Mitchell, S.W.; 142
Mitchell, Wiley; 157
Mobley, Mrs. J.B.; 129
Moore, Jesse H.; 136
Morrison, Fannie Wyche; 126
Mulloy, Edna; 123
Mulloy, J. W.; 30, 52, 123
Mulloy, Jim; 52, 123
Mulloy, Joe; 123
Mulloy, Pat; 52
Mulloy, Sarah Louise; 30
New Braunfels, Texas; 148-150
Nunn, Mrs. G. J.; 5
Orr, Sula; 7
Overland Trail; 33
Owens, Jim; 127
Ozona, Texas; 31, 43, 79
Parker, Quanah; 62
Paxton, J.F.; 142
Payne, Jack; 10
Pearce, John; 12
Pearce, Miss Ollie; 156
Permien, Ludwig; 144
Peters, Bud; 143
Peters, S.E.; 143
Pevyhouse, Hattie; 127
Poulson, Mrs. Annie; 143
Powers, Andrew Jackson; 74, 128
Powers, Elijah; 128
Powers, Francis; 128
Powers, Frank; 128
Powers, Joe; 128

Index

Powers, John; 128
Powers, Lewis B.; 128
Powers, Mrs. Lizzie; 53, 74, 93, 126
Powers, Sam; 127
Powers, Tom; 128
Powers, William; 128
Prince, Bob; 95
Quigley, W.B.; 6
Quitaque Ranch; 38
Randal, Mrs. Fayette; 2, 42
Rau, Otto; 146
Reynolds, Ada; 10
Reynolds, Mrs. Ben; 9
Rice, Dr. S.P.; 143
Richard, I.R.; 143
Richardson, Lizzie; 158
Riesel, Texas; 53, 144, 149
Roberts, Joel; 160
Robinson Creek; 70
Roe, Elizabeth; 18, 49, 57, 75
Roe, Montgomery; 49
Russell, J.L.; 140
Russell, Mrs. Cicero; 41, 65
Rylee, Mrs. J. D.; 40, 67, 75, 80
Sabinal, Texas; 35, 72, 83
San Angelo, Texas; 2, 27, 41, 42, 47, 65, 68, 77, 80
San Antonio, Texas; 3, 9, 35, 54
Sanborn, Henry B.; 8
Sanders, Rev. Liff; 130
Sandlin, Joe; 160
Sanford, Becky; 27, 42
Scharlach, Mrs. John; 150
Schimmelpfennig, Hermann; 148
Schmidt, John; 147
Schmidt, Mrs. L.H.; 146
Schneider, Rev. Eduard; 148
Schoonover, Sol; 42
Schreiner, Capt. Charles; 2
Seely or Sealy, Paul; 37
Shaw, Mrs. Annie; 9, 54
Shaw, Sam; 12
Sheets, Jesse; 45

Shelton, Mamie; 127
Shelton, Pines; 128
Shipley, Mrs. D.D.; 103
Siemering, August; 147
Slaughter, C.C.; 130
Smith, Bill; 19
Smith, C.S.; 25
Smith, Dr. R.L.; 12
Smith, H.C.; 142
Smith, Hank; 38, 96, 98
Smyth brothers; 156
Snodgrass, James; 143
Sommerville, Mark; 157
Sommerville, Phoebe; 157
Squaw Creek; 68
St. Helen, John; 40
Starks, J.D.; 113
Stephens, Clarence; 127
Stephens, Lewis; 10
Stockett, John & Henry; 114
Stodghill, W.B.; 12, 128
Stone, Dewitt; 160
Storey, Bruce; 140
Storey, George; 140
Storey, J.D.; 140
Storey, J.W.; 143
Stranger, Texas; 157
Suttle family; 11, 12, 127
Swarts, C.L.; 137
Swinnea, Jim; 160
Tascosa, Texas; 16, 44
Tate, Mrs. Mollie; 158
Taylor, William; 153
Tenney, Rev. L.; 142
Thomas, Mary Wyche; 126
Tidwell, George; 127
Timmons, Bascom; 7
Twichell, Eula Trigg; 122
Twichell, W.D.; 16, 122
Upshaw outlaws; 40, 44
Uvalde, Texas; 35, 41, 47, 71, 72, 83, 105, 109
Valley, Frank; 44
Vance, Mrs. Hattie; 1

Vann, Ed; 162
Vaughan family; 11, 127
Vaughan, H.T.; 128
Vickers, Ernest; 157
Waco, Texas; 2, 10, 13, 42, 50, 59, 123
Waite, Mary Powers; 128
Waite, Mrs. Joe; 143
Waite, William; 128
Walker, Abner; 46
Walker, J.A.; 142
Walker, William C.; 2
Wallace, Bigfoot; 50
Ward, Mrs. Mary Jane; 45
Weathers, J.P.; 139
Weathers, Tom; 26
Weiss, August; 53
Weiss, Frederich; 150
Weiss, Fritz; 53
Weiss, Louis; 150
White, Mrs. A. E.; 23
Whitesides, Dr. R.B.; 140, 143
Wichita Falls, Texas; 29, 62, 114
Williams, Katy; 65
Williams, Milton; 84
Williams, Nancy; 84
Williams, Robert; 84
Williams, W.R.; 156
Willis, Judge J.D.; 16
Willis, Mrs. M.B.; 13
Winn, J.W.; 131
Witting, Mrs. Fred; 150
Wolffarth, Mrs. George C.; 37
Woodward, Wm. & Elizabeth; 9, 54
Wright, Annie; 143
Wright, Mrs. T.F.; 24
Wright, Sue; 143
Wyche, Dr. George; 53, 126
Wyche, Eugene; 126
Wyche, Fannie; 126
Wyche, Fred; 126
Wyche, James; 126
Wyche, Laura; 126
Wyche, Mr. Beverly; 126
Young family; 127
Younger boys; 40, 42